HEDGES

Loving Your Marriage Enough to Protect It

Jerry B. Jenkins

Wolgemuth & Hyatt, Publishers, Inc.
Brentwood, Tennessee

Wolgemuth & Hyatt, Publishers, Inc. is a commercial information packager whose mission is to publish and distribute books that lead individuals toward:

- A personal faith in the one true God: Father, Son, and Holy Spirit;
- A lifestyle of practical discipleship; and
- A worldview that is consistent with the historic, Christian faith.

Moreover, the company endeavors to accomplish this mission at a reasonable profit and in a manner which glorifies God and serves His Kingdom.

Published November 1989. First Edition
Printed in the United States of America
96 95 94 93 92 91 90 89 8 7 6 5 4 3 2 1

Wolgemuth & Hyatt, Publishers, Inc.
1749 Mallory Lane, Suite 110, Brentwood, Tennessee 37027.

Library of Congress Cataloging-in-Publication Data

Jenkins, Jerry B.
Hedges : loving your marriage enough to protect it / Jerry B. Jenkins. — 1st ed.
p. cm.
ISBN 0-943497-40-X : $14.95
1. Marriage—Religious aspects—Christianity. I. Title.
BV835.J46 1989
248.8'44—dc20 89-38488
CIP

To Dianna, of course

CONTENTS

INTRODUCTION

A GIFT OF LOVE

One of the major causes of marital breakups in the Christian community is the lack of protective hedges that spouses should plant around their marriages, their heads, their hearts, their eyes, and their hands.

Writing "Of Scandals and Hedges" in my magazine column bordered on being too personal. It concerned what we must do to protect our marriages from infidelity, and I worried that it might be more embarrassing than helpful—to the reader and to me.

Here are some excerpts from that column:

> Someone asked recently why I had not devoted a column to The [PTL] Scandal. I wish I could have said that enough had written enough about enough, but were it not for how far in advance one has to write for a periodical such as this, I'd have likely been on the bandwagon.

Rather than rehash the pain . . . maybe there's value in reviewing the hedges we Christians must build around our marriages. I have a list of rather prudish rules that I used to be embarrassed to speak of—except to my wife, to whom they are a gift of love.

They are intended to protect my eyes, my heart, my hands, and therefore my marriage. I direct the rules toward appearances and find that if you take care of how things look, you take care of how they are. In other words, if you are never alone with an unrelated female, because it might not look appropriate, you have eliminated the possibility that anything inappropriate will take place.

I say these rules appear prudish because my mentioning them when necessary has elicited squints, scowls, and not-so-hidden smiles of condescension. And in outlining them here, I risk implying that without following my list, I would immediately be plunged into all manner of affairs.

In enforcing my own rules I don't mean to insult the many virtuous women who might otherwise have very legitimate reasons to meet or dine with me without the slightest temptation to have designs on me.

Simply hedges, that's all these rules are. And much as people don't like to hear, read, or talk about it, the fact is that most Christian men do not have victory over lust. I have a theory about that. Scripture does not imply that we ever shall have victory over lust the way we are expected to win over worry or greed or malice. Rather, Paul instructs Timothy, and thus us, not to conquer or stand and fight, or pray about or resolve, but to *flee* lust.

> I know he specifies *youthful* lust, but I don't believe he is limiting it to a certain age, but rather is describing it, regardless at what age it occurs. The little boy in me, and I have room for several, will have to flee lust until I flee life. (*Moody Monthly*, July/August 1987. Used by permission)

I then shared the six hedges I build around myself to protect me, my wife, my family, my employer, my church, and supremely, the reputation of Christ. I shared them not to boast, but to admit that I'm still fleeing and in the hope that there be some benefit to someone.

I was afraid I had been too open, too vulnerable, but that proved unfounded. I received more mail and comment about that column than anything I'd ever written. Clearly, the idea had struck a chord. People asked for more on the subject.

But I'm a layman, a writer—not a Bible scholar, psychologist, or counselor. That, some told me, was why I should expand on the subject.

"Be sure it's Bible-based, of course, but not heavily theological. And leave the psychology to the experts. Emphasize the practical. Provide handles, something to grab on to, something a person can *do* to protect a marriage."

This book is a result of that challenge and of the belief in the project on the parts of the publishers.

❧ Jerry B. Jenkins
Beach Park, Illinois

PART ONE

THE NEED FOR HEDGES

No one thinks he needs hedges until it's too late.

ONE

THE TANGLED WEB

Sexual immorality hits frighteningly close to home. Without being aware of the need to protect ourselves against it, we are vulnerable.

Sue was not the prettiest and certainly not the sexiest woman John had ever seen. In fact, she didn't hold a candle to his wife. But Sue worked for John. He spent a lot of time with her at the office. He could tell she admired him. He liked her, respected her, and thought she was bright, creative, and interesting. He liked being around her, liked her smile, enjoyed her wit. She was doe-eyed, had perfect teeth, and was married.

Was John romantically interested in her? The question would have offended him. They were both happily married. They didn't even think about an attraction between them. John told his wife about Sue from the day she was hired. His wife was eager to meet Sue and her husband, and the couples genuinely liked each other. The couples didn't socialize frequently because they lived too far from each other, but Sue kept John up to date on what was happening in her life, and John told his wife. Sue and John's wife talked on the phone occasionally. John wasn't starry-eyed about Sue, and John's wife had no reason to believe Sue held anything for John but respect.

Which was true.

Was Sue worth losing a home and family? Now there was a question even more insulting than the first. No woman was worth that. In fact, John used to tease his wife, "If I ever throw you over, kid, at least I won't humiliate you by running off with a dog."

It was a joke, because it was the last thing on his mind. He was a Christian, active in church, a father of three, a baby-boomer with a comfortable and happy life. He wasn't looking for anything more or different. He was challenged, motivated, and excited about his job and his career path. He was solid. John wasn't even going through a mid-life crisis.

So he didn't worry when he first found himself missing Sue when she was out of town for a couple of days. He asked his secretary to be sure to let him know when she called, because he had "business to discuss with her." It was true. And when the business had been discussed, they talked a little more.

"We miss you around here, Sue." The emphasis was on "we."

"I miss you too," she said. "All of you. Look forward to seeing you when I get back."

"Me too."

Nice. Friendly. Innocent. Dangerous. But John didn't know that then.

When Sue returned, her relationship with John changed in subtle ways. In a meeting or a room full of people they could read each other's eyes in an instant. They weren't reading anything personal. They just knew what the other was thinking about the topic at hand. John could tell when Sue was hedging, being circumspect. Sue could tell when John was just being polite, when he didn't really like a proposal but was kind in how he responded to it.

John began to find reasons to be around Sue. He also found reasons to touch her in a brotherly or even fatherly way—a squeeze of the hand, a touch on the shoulder, a hug of greeting or farewell. He would not have described it as sexual or even sensual, any more than any man would enjoy physical contact with an attractive young female.

John was waiting for a cab to the airport as Sue left the office for the day. "The airport's on my way home," she reminded him. "I'll give you a ride."

They talked business on the way. At the curb he looked into her eyes and thanked her warmly. "Any time," she said. "Anything for you." He held her gaze for a moment until the humor of her comment sank in. They both smiled. "You know what I mean," she added.

"Of course."

They both knew she meant she would do anything proper for such a good friend. But both also liked the intimate sound of words that could be taken a variety of ways.

In the ensuing weeks and months, John and Sue began slowly to depend upon each other emotionally. He told her things no one else in the office knew: his dreams, plans, private ambitions, his assessments of others. They went from telling each other what good friends they were to making their conversation more personal, more meaningful. He called her his "favorite friend." She often told him he was "special."

Theirs wasn't a typical dual pity party, each bad-mouthing his own spouse and looking to the other for ingredients missing in the marriages. No, this was simply a case of two people who hit it off, liked each other, became special to each other, and eventually became enamored with each other. Suddenly, or so it seemed, the inevitable happened.

They justified a few lunches and even a working dinner. When their bodies touched while sitting in a cab or in a restaurant booth, neither pulled away. It was natural, familiar. Brotherly and sisterly. When he touched her arm while talking to her, he often left his hand there even after his point had been made.

At a convention out of town, even with six others from their office along, they found opportunities to be alone together. It wasn't easy, but though their relationship had not escalated to the declaring stage yet, they both knew. There was no one either would rather be with. After a late dinner with everyone from their office, she called his room and said she couldn't sleep.

"I'm not tired either," he lied. He had collapsed into bed after the long day. "What do you want to do?"

"I don't know. Just talk."

"So talk."

"You wanna go for a walk?"

"Sure."

They met in the lobby and strolled the deserted city streets. She thought her sweater would be enough, but the summer night grew chilly after midnight, and as they crossed a bridge over the river, he slipped his suit jacket over her shoulders. She smiled at him in the moonlight, and he put his arm around her. She slipped her hand around his waist. They walked silently for twenty minutes until they came to a dark spot between street lights.

John slowed to a stop, his emotions racing. Sue looked quizzically at him, but when he took her in his arms, they embraced so naturally, so perfectly that it seemed right. He could feel her heart pounding. "Dare I kiss you?" he whispered in her hair.

She held him tighter, as if stalling to decide. "It's your call," she said, mimicking his favorite expression to subordinates when insisting they make their own decisions. It was all he needed to hear.

Theirs was one long, soft, meaningful kiss that spoke volumes. They stared into each other's eyes for a slow moment, then headed back to the hotel, his hand gently on her arm. As the building came into sight, Sue stopped. "We have to talk," she said.

"I know."

"What are you thinking, John?"

"The same thing you're thinking."

"Don't be too sure."

"I'm sure, Sue. I'll be shocked if you're not thinking what I think you're thinking."

"You first, Boss."

"This will never work, Sue. It didn't happen. We go back to our respective rooms good friends, good associates, two people who happen to like each other very much."

Her eyes filled. "You know me too well."

"I'm relieved to hear you say that, Sue. I certainly didn't intend this, and I don't want to mislead you."

"The walk was my idea, but I didn't have this is mind either."

"Nothing happened, Sue. Deal?" He stuck out his hand.

She shook it but held on. "Why do I want to kiss you again, John? I agree we have to end this, but it seems so incomplete."

"I feel the same way. But we cannot. We must not."

"I know," she said, dropping his hand.

She thanked him for the use of his coat and smiled bravely at him as she left the elevator at her floor.

John stared at the ceiling until four in the morning, dredging up every negative detail of his marriage. In twelve years he and his wife had become known as a successful and happily married couple. By the time he gave up trying to sleep, however, he had convinced himself that he had never loved her, that the marriage was a mistake, and that he felt something for Sue he had never felt for any other woman, including—and especially—his wife.

His jaw set and his mind whirling, John strode to the window and gazed into the darkness. Was that a person sitting on the low concrete wall in the courtyard below? As John watched, the figure moved. It was a woman, and as he studied her, he knew it was Sue.

John freshened up and dressed quickly. He took the stairs all the way to the ground floor and exited a side door unnoticed. Sue started when she first saw him, then she sat still and stared ahead resignedly, as if this new meeting were somehow inevitable. John stood before her. "Sue, are you all right?"

She nodded and dabbed at her face with a tissue. "I just have to get over this," she said.

"Anything I can do?"

She shook her head. "It's not going to be easy working with you."

"It doesn't have to be difficult, Sue. We just need to back up a few months. We're good friends, and we can enjoy that, can't we?"

"You make the let's-be-friends routine sound easy, John. I can't."

"Why not?"

She took a deep, quavery breath and fought for composure. She hadn't looked at him since he first approached. "I'm in love with you, John. That's why."

He reached for her and she came to him. They embraced and kissed, and he told her he loved her, too. He led her back into the hotel the way he'd come, avoiding the lobby and the elevators. They trudged up the stairs to her room. He left there two hours later, in time to prepare for the day.

John and Sue shared a delicious, bleary-eyed secret for the rest of the convention. They spent most of every night together, and there was no more talk of how things would have to change when they traveled back home to reality.

John and Sue convinced themselves that their love was so perfect that God had to be in it. Neither was prepared for the vehement reactions from their spouses and their extended families. The anger, the confusion, the accusations drove them closer to each other. Within six months both divorces were final, and John and Sue were married. A year later, while Sue was pregnant with her first child, John announced that he had made a terrible mistake. He wanted his wife and family back, and he set upon such an impractical and obnoxious approach that he lost his job and his new wife. In the process he permanently alienated himself from his former wife as well.

Surely Not Them!

John and Sue's story is representative of several I've heard from friends, relatives, and acquaintances. It has become so common that I cringe when someone says, "Did you hear about so-and-so?" They may be informing me of a move or a new job or a new baby, but my first dreaded thought is, *Oh, no, please, not them too.* All too often, my worst fears are confirmed. No one is immune. The strongest marriage you know of is in danger today if hedges are not in place.

Not long ago I reminisced with several old friends. What a shocking disappointment to discover that every one of us knew personally of at least one painful marriage failure due to infidelity. Even more appalling, nearly all of us could point to incidents among our close relatives. Can anyone still doubt that the sexual revolution has brought about an epidemic of divorce?

In a strange way, the problem is exacerbated in the Christian community because unfaithful spouses are generally not in danger—the way the secular community is—of contracting AIDS or herpes. The type of a person I'm writing about is not characteristically promiscuous. John, in the above example, had never before slept with a woman other than his wife. Ironically, while the secular world is cleaning up its act due to fear of deadly disease, Christians blithely proceed, unaware they need hedges to keep them from surprise attacks in their areas of sexual weakness.

Try an informal survey on your own. Ask friends and relatives if they know people who have fallen to sexual temptation. Perhaps you don't need to ask. Maybe you know firsthand more such stories than you care to recount. And if the people involved were vulnerable, who else might be? Who will be the next one about whom you say, "I never would have dreamed he would do such a thing"? You know these people, and you have to wonder what made them fall. What made them vulnerable?

The Little Foxes

Just as it's the little foxes who spoil the vine, so the seemingly small indiscretions add up to major traps. John and Sue allowed themselves to admire, like, respect, and enjoy each other without giving a second thought to the progression of feelings, the danger of developing emotional feelings, the lure of infatuation. They never reminded themselves of their wedding vows because they had no intention of breaking them. Feelings and emotions sneaked up on them when they least expected it, and then it was too late.

Look at the Biblical account of David's failure in 2 Samuel, chapter eleven. Here was a man after God's own heart. Have you ever wondered why he didn't go to battle? Scripture doesn't provide a lot of detail about this incident, but the question arises: Was David too old, too tired, too successful, or too something to lead his army? Or was there some subconscious, or not so subconscious, maneuvering to get himself into a position where he could have an opportunity to get next to Uriah's wife?

Why did he take a walk on his veranda that day? Was Bathsheba not aware that her bath was within the line of sight from the king's palace? It's fair to say that an innocent walk and a bath in the open air could be considered nearly innocent indiscretions. Give Bathsheba the benefit of the doubt, and David should have turned away when saw a naked woman. The fact that even a man after God's own heart was unable to do that lends credence to my theory that we are to flee rather than to try to conquer lust.

Inviting the wife of your commanding officer over after seeing her bathe must be considered more than a small indiscretion. Even in my respect for a man of God, I have to suspect David's motives. Could he simply have wanted to get better acquainted? Indeed! He knew this woman. Surely she was known in the social circles of the government, being married to a high-ranking soldier and living within sight of the palace. Did David know when he invited her that he would sleep with her that night? Surely he wasn't testing his resolve to remain pure before God. What Bathsheba knew or didn't know we can scarcely guess. In that time, a summons from the king was disobeyed only under the threat of death, so from the time she received his invitation, her fate was sealed.

Safe to say, had it not been for the initial indiscretions, adultery may never have resulted. And look at what happened after that. Bathsheba became pregnant. David called Uriah home from battle in the hope that he would sleep with his wife and believe the child was his own. Uriah, a man of honor (how that must have made David feel!), refused to enjoy the comforts of his home and his wife while his men were engaged in battle. Had Uriah slept with his wife, David would have fostered deceit. As it turned out, Uriah's sense of duty drove David to have him killed. Scripture tells how David sent the Hittite back to war with his own death notice in his hand (2 Samuel 11:14–15).

Encounters of the Too Close Kind

How close have you come to being burned? Have you found yourself impressed with someone and then attracted to them? Maybe it seemed innocent and safe, but then you said or did things you never thought you would say or do. Maybe on a business trip you hung around with a colleague of the opposite sex, and upon reflection you know you wouldn't have wanted your spouse to do the same thing. It could be that nothing improper was said or done, but simply investing the emotional energy and time was inappropriate. Maybe, looking back, you can see that you were living dangerously. When friends fall right and left, you see that perhaps you were lucky you weren't snared.

Or maybe you did become emotionally or even physically involved and fell just short of actually committing adultery. Perhaps you live with guilt because you never confided that to anyone, including—and especially—your spouse.

If so many of your friends and acquaintances have fallen—people you never would have suspected—how will you avoid being a casualty?

TWO

THE CHANGING CLIMATE

There's a new openness in society to interaction between the sexes in the workplace, in the neighborhood, in counseling, and even in the church. Christians touch more, speak more intimately, and are closer to one another than ever. There are advantages, but there are also grave dangers. Fear can be good, a catalyst for action. Fear is as good a motivator as any to maintain fidelity.

According to a survey conducted by Christianity Today, Inc. researchers, of one thousand readers (non-pastors) of *Christianity Today*, fully 23 percent indicated they had engaged in sexual intercourse with someone other than their wives. Twenty-eight percent indicated they had involved themselves in other forms of sexual contact outside their marriages. In a separate survey of pastors, 23 percent said they had done something sexually inappropriate outside their marriages, 12 percent indicating adulterous intercourse.*

What could John and Sue have done to insure against the misery they brought upon themselves? Such second marriages seldom work, but make no mistake, had their marriage been idyllic, it would still have been disastrous for their previous spouses, John's children, and both extended families.

First, both should have been aware of the potential danger and recognized the infatuation for what it was. This is basic, though not admitted to by most Christians. It simply is not uncommon in the workplace to meet someone with whom there seems an immediate bonding. You like them, they like you, you hit it off. *That* is the time to deal with the problem, because it can become a serious dilemma.

You can be married ten years and still develop a crush on someone. You think about them, find yourself talking about them, quoting them (even to your spouse), and generally becoming enamored with them. The Christianity Today, Inc. survey showed clearly that the major factor contributing to extramarital relationships is physical and emotional attraction (78 percent), far outdistancing marital dissatisfaction (41 percent).†

That is the time to remind yourself that this is nothing more than an adult version of adolescent puppy love, and it will pass. It really will. The person is off limits, and

---

* "How Common Is Pastoral Indiscretion?" *Leadership* (Winter 1988): 12–13.

† Ibid., 13.

you should run from the situation as from a contagious disease.

You may still see the person in the work setting, and you may still enjoy proper interaction with them. But ground rules need to be set. Never tell the person that you are attracted to them. Talk about your spouse frequently in front of them. Tell your spouse about the person, but use your own judgment as to how fully to explain your dilemma. I have a friend who seems to delight in telling his wife about all the women upon whom he develops such instant and fleeting crushes. He encourages her to do the same, but while she admits she is susceptible to similar experiences, she prefers not to talk about them or to hear about his. My own wife is fully aware of my hedges, and thus she is not threatened by my extolling the appropriate virtues of an associate. Of course I don't rhapsodize about someone's looks or say stupid things like, "If I had met her before I met you . . ."

When you first become aware of the impact the other person has on you, that is the time to move into action. You should be able to determine the extent of the danger a person represents to you by your own body language, how you sit or stand when talking with them, how much eye contact seems acceptable, whether you seem magnetized by them, and how much you look forward to seeing them.

Don't treat your new friend the way you treat an old, respected friend. Refrain from touching them, being alone with them, flirting with them (even in jest), or saying anything to them you wouldn't say if your spouse were there. (While you may not be so rigid in your conduct with a long-time friend of the opposite sex, beware. Certain guidelines must be enforced. Friendships, especially with long-admired associates, can turn into something more intimate even more quickly than new alliances.)

So, what could John and Sue have done? Had either realized they were becoming enamored with each other, they could have shifted gears, gone into a protective mode, and saved themselves from ruining many lives.

If hedges are constructed early enough, preferably well in advance of even meeting someone else, they can be painless and can nip marriage-threatening relationships before they get started. That's the reason we so desperately need practical suggestions on ways to build impenetrable hedges around our marriages.

If you can believe *The Hite Report on Male Sexuality*,* which I don't recommend reading or believing, nearly three-fourths of married men cheat on their wives. Admittedly, the responses are from people with enough interest in the subject to answer a multi-page questionnaire which gave them the opportunity to discuss sex in the most pedestrian and vulgar terms, generally robbing it of any sacred mystery. In fact, the monumental report itself (1,129 pages in hardback) could be enlisted as a masturbatory aid, if one was so inclined. A huge percentage of the respondents appear so inclined, as evidenced in their comments.

On the subject of adultery, the author summarizes:

> The great majority of married men were not monogamous. Seventy-two percent of men married two years or more had had sex outside of marriage: the over-

---

* See Shere Hite, *The Hite Report On Male Sexuality* (New York: Alfred A. Knopf, 1981).

> whelming majority did not tell their wives, at least at the time [of the incidents].*

Given the unscientific, non-representative nature of the research, the above quotation can be taken with a healthy dose of sodium, but it should be pointed out that a significant number of respondents referred to themselves as born-again Christians. Putting this body of research with the Christianity Today, Inc. survey provides a rough idea where the Christian community fits in the overall scheme of marital faithfulness.

When a famous television evangelist announced he was stepping aside from his ministry because of an affair, I shook my head. I had never been a follower of the man, but I had been bemused by what appeared to be a confused set of values. Sadly, the news of his moral failure was thus not a surprise. Further revelations included gross financial mismanagement, empire building, and even homosexuality.

Another Christian television personality's moral failure included a lifelong fascination with pornography and an apparent attempt to get as close as possible to extramarital sex without actually committing it.

Hearing the stories of the ruined ministries of television evangelists due to sexual immorality is one thing. Seeing the same thing happen to your neighbor, your friend, or a family member is something else altogether. It may be hard to identify with the man who has everything—a ministry, wealth, status, popularity, a beautiful family—and risks it all for a season of pleasure, but it is not hard to identify with the man next door.

---

* Ibid.

When your assistant pastor, brother-in-law, or best friend from college falls, that's too close to home. Then you get to see at close range the tumble of dominoes set in motion by infidelity.

The Price of Infidelity

Infidelity. What a genteel word for the act it describes. Such a word goes down easier than violating one's trust, breaking one's marriage vows, being unfaithful, sleeping around, fornicating, committing adultery. But using a mild word for sin doesn't change a thing.

I was twelve years old when I was first affected by the ravages of immorality. Something was wrong in the only church I had ever known, and no one would tell me what was going on. There were meetings, public and private, charges, accusations, arguments, tears, factions. I badgered and bugged and bothered until I forced my mother to tell me what I really didn't want to know.

"You're too young to deal with it."

"No I'm not, Mom. I'm twelve!" How old that sounded at the time!

"You'll wish you hadn't asked."

"Just tell me! Please!"

"You wouldn't believe it."

"Yes, I will! Tell me!"

"Would you believe me if I told you that our pastor doesn't love his wife anymore?"

"No!"

"See?"

It couldn't be true. The pastor and his wife were perfect! They had four of their own children and had adopted another. I had looked up to and admired and respected them for as long as I could remember. A young married woman in the church had been the center of the rumors. Was there an affair? Had someone seen them embrace? Could the stories be true of the pastor berating his wife? My head swam as the rumors flew around our church.

The pastor's final sermon was a not-so-veiled admission of a mistake he had made years before—his choice of a wife. The church was ravaged by a near-split soon after his departure. Then came the news of the divorce. His ministry was over. That little church was left in pieces, and it took years to pull itself back together.

I thought no such trauma had ever before hit a wonderful church like ours, nor could it ever happen again. Since then I have heard countless such stories, including both a senior pastor and an assistant pastor I had sat under. One left notes for his trusted friends and associates, praising God for "this new, divine love that is so wonderful that He had to author it." Another friend tried to convince me that the relationship that broke up both his and his girlfriend's marriages was "in the center of God's will."

The Underlying Root

What seemed an aberration more than twenty-five years ago in a small town was merely a harbinger for the marital devastation that has hit the Christian community today.

Marriages are breaking up at such an alarming rate that it's hard to find someone who has not been affected by divorce in his immediate family. How many divorces can you count in your own family, including grandparents on both sides, aunts, uncles, and your own siblings?

You may not know how many of those divorces were the result of immorality, but half is a fair assumption. Women leave their husbands for a variety of complex reasons, the most minor of which—according to marriage counselors—is their own lust. Rarely do you hear of a woman who simply fell for someone who, by his sexual appeal alone, turned her head and heart from her own husband.

But men—yes, even those who would blame their frumpy, crabby, boring wives for their own roving eyes—don't really need an excuse. They will point to myriad reasons for having to leave, but it nearly always can be traced to lust, pride, and a false sense of their own strength. Remember that the major factors leading to the illicit relationships in the Christianity Today, Inc. survey showed 78 percent of respondents citing physical and emotional attraction while only 41 percent cited marital dissatisfaction.*

Think of the men you know and the reasons they gave for finding someone new. Did some of them have incredibly attractive, even sexy wives? Can all those men complain of their wives' frigidity?

A strange aspect of infidelity is that a man usually has to invent reasons after the fact. The man who once taught marriage seminars, raved about his wife, treated her right, was proud of her, now must say:

"We hid the truth. Our marriage was never good."

"In private she was not what she appeared to be in public."

"I never loved her."

---

* "How Common is Pastoral Indescretion?" 13.

"She didn't understand me" (the oldest saw in the tool kit).

No Excuse

We all know the adage that every broken marriage has two sides and that there's no such thing as a completely innocent party. However, those statements need examination. No, none of us knows what went on behind closed doors, and we all know how base we can be in private, compared to the image we like to project in public.

But if you know divorced couples, you know of examples where, if she was not innocent, the wife was certainly not guilty of anything that justified her husband's leaving her for another woman. I've been acquainted with enough such offending men to see their defenses coming a mile away. Suddenly this woman we all know as a wonderful person—not perfect, maybe a bit dull, maybe harried and overworked, maybe not as dazzling as she was when they first married—is painted as a monster. This from the man who is no prize himself, yet he has justified breaking the laws of God, breaking his promises to his wife, violating their union, and blaming it on her! I once knew a denominational leader in his sixties who carried on a year-long affair with a younger woman. When he was exposed and defrocked and called before his superiors, he brought along his wife who took full responsibility. No confession. No apology. It was her fault, he said. She said it herself.

Call it what you will, but a man with as perfect a wife as he could ever want is still capable of lust, of a senseless seeking of that which would destroy him and his family. If he does not fear his own potential and build a hedge around himself and his marriage, he heads for disaster.

A Healthy Fear

Shall we all run scared? Yes! Fear is essential. "There are several good protections against temptation," Mark Twain said, "but the surest is cowardice."*

Look around. Let your guard down, don't remind yourself that you made a vow before God and men, don't set up barriers for your eyes, your mind, your hands, your emotions, and see how quickly you become a statistic.

A man may say, "It could never happen to me. I love my wife. We know each other inside out by now. We've left the emotional infatuation stage that ruled our courtship and honeymoon, and we love God's way: unconditionally and by the act of our wills. We each know the other is not perfect and we accept and love each other anyway. We're invulnerable to attack, especially by lust that leads to immorality."

But when—because he has not planted hedges to protect himself—he falls, his tune changes. Then his excuse is that he fell out of love, the old magic was no longer there, the wife was too busy with the house and kids, his needs were not fulfilled at home.

Worse, the Christian deserter becomes so infatuated with his new love that he often gives God the credit. Know a counseling pastor or a Christian psychologist? Ask him how many times he's heard a man say, "This new relationship is so beautiful, God has to be behind it." Never mind that it goes against all sense and every tenet of Scripture, not to mention everything the man has ever believed in and stood for.

---

* Mark Twain, *Following the Equator,* vol. I, "Pudd'nhead Wilson's New Calendar," ch. 36.

What is happening? When we baby-boomers were in elementary school we knew one, maybe two kids from broken homes. Divorce among church people was almost nonexistent. Now the solid, happy marriage is the exception. From people we never dreamed would have problems come stories of affairs, adultery, separation, and divorce.

This is not the forum in which to debate the issue of divorce. Scripture is clear that God hates divorce (Malachi 2:16), but opinions vary as to whether He forbids it altogether or allows it in only one or two circumstances, and whether remarriage is allowed regardless of the reason for the divorce.

No matter where you stand on those issues, you must agree that no one marries intending or wanting to divorce. Some, no doubt, from the beginning consider divorce a convenient option and vow to stay together for as long as we both shall *love*. But even the Christian with the most liberal position possible on divorce says and means at his wedding that he is pledging himself to his wife forever. He may later forget it or decide that it was merely archaic formality, but there's no way around it. His vows were legal, sacred, and moral. When he commits adultery, he breaks his promise.

One of the most effective ways to deal with a friend who is trying to justify his adultery is to say, "Bill, don't forget that I was there. I heard you say it. I heard you promise that you would take no one but Jane unto yourself for as long as you both shall live."

"Yeah, but—"

"You can 'yeah, but' all you want, but the fact is, you broke your promise."

"But she—"

"Regardless what *she* did or didn't do, *you* broke *your* promise, didn't you?"

That can take the wind out of any sail made of excuses.

Run, Don't Walk

A complex litany of events takes place between the vows and the adultery, and it behooves those of us who want to remain pure to examine those events, expose them for what they are, and either avoid letting them happen or avoid letting Satan use them to trick us into justifying our sin.

Once we have identified them, what will we do about them? Will we pray over them? Resolve to conquer them? Turn over new leaves? Ironically, the answer is easier than that. We are not to win, not to gain the victory, not to succeed by the sheer force of our wills, our consciences, or our determination.

> Flee the evil desires of youth, and pursue righteousness, faith, love and peace, along with those who call on the Lord out of a pure heart. (2 Timothy 2:22, New International Version)

We are to run. To flee. To get out. To get away. Why? Does this admonition to flee somehow serve as an admission on God's part that He did not even equip us with the ability to subdue our natures in this area? The question is valid. Of adultery, in the Old Testament God tells us, "You shall not" (Exodus 20:14), and in the New Testament He says that if we so much as look upon a woman to lust after her, we have already committed adultery with her in our hearts (Matthew 5:28).

In other areas, God grants us victory. We can win over jealousy, a bad temper, greed, and even pride. We can train our consciences to avoid theft, bad mouthing, and lying. But who do you know who could avoid a peek at pornography if convinced no one would find out?

Clearly there are times when we are stronger than at other times. So what is the solution when temptation rages? If we are weak and have not taken precautions, if we have not applied preventive medicine, we have already failed. The only answer is to plan, to anticipate danger, to plot the way of escape.

The time to build hedges is before the enemy attacks.

THREE

DON'T BLAME GOD

One of the most fascinating and misunderstood differences between men and women is in their thought processes and sexual triggers.

I was in the eighth grade when short skirts became popular. I thought I'd died and gone to heaven. Our school went through ninth grade, so to me ninth-grade girls were WOMEN. Of course, in 1962–63, what I considered short skirts were just an inch or two above the knee. Lord, have mercy! The trend would escalate to micro minis by the time I reached college, so I spent my entire adolescence with my eyes open.

I suppose that era made me a leg man, though it would be a lie to say that any other female physical attribute is far down my appreciation list. Lest I sound like a wolf-whistling lecher, please know that this was a private sport. While we junior high boys might nudge someone so he could follow our eyes to a choice target, for some reason we didn't admit to each other how deeply we felt about looking at girls.

Indeed, I thought I was probably the only Christian boy attracted to the female figure. From childhood I had read in a denominational magazine letters from teen-agers lamenting having gone too far in their relationships and pleading for advice on how to control themselves. That turned out to be a good foundation for me when I began dating and facing temptation. I credit that early input—along with dating virtuous women—for coming to my wedding night as virginal as my bride: wholly.

Yet in junior high and high school I feared I would wind up as one of those letter writers. I was so enamored with women and their sensual beauty that I was convinced I had the potential to become a fiend. When I realized that even more exciting to me than any sports drama was watching a girl cross her legs and catching a glimpse of thigh, I knew I had it bad.

Had I only known this was normal! That I was not alone! That such attraction to women, yes, even to their sexuality, was God's idea! Is that heresy? It's not now, and it wasn't then. Though I can't recall having purely lustful thoughts in junior high, I carried a deep sense of guilt about even *wanting* to look at girls. As best I can recall, I had no thoughts of illicit sex. Still, I felt guilty. Something seemed wrong with thinking about this all the time. What a relief it would have been to discover that (depending on which expert you read) the typical American adolescent male thinks about sex no fewer than four times every minute!

Of course, as I graduated from puberty and went on for a master's degree in girl watching, it became more and more difficult to separate looking and appreciating from lusting. It was of only small comfort to me when I heard a Christian youth leader say that 99 percent of all heterosexual boys have a problem with lust and that the other 1 percent are liars. I was devout in my faith and knew right from wrong, yet I seemed to have no control, no resolve, no victory in this area. I regret not having had an adult perspective that would have allowed me to enjoy those years with wonder and without guilt.

With my own three boys, one of whom—Dallas—is a young teen, I already allow for the natural attraction to and preoccupation with females, and we talk about it rather than pretend there's something wrong with it. I sometimes caution Dallas about thoughts, and we discuss openly the priceless value of his goal to reach marriage without having fallen into sexual sin.

Beyond that I don't pretend that he should chastise himself for appreciating a form designed by God to attract him. Without being crude, we discuss which girl in an ad or on a television program is most attractive and why. I admit that women are still fun to look at, even at my ripe age (forty). Dallas probably gets tired of my cautioning him to be careful about dwelling on the sexual and to simply admire, delight in, enjoy, and respect God's beautiful creativity.

Drs. Miriam and Otto Ehrenberg classify parents in four categories according to their views of sex in raising their children: Sex Repressive (sex is bad and should be discussed or dealt with only in that light), Sex Avoidant (sex is okay but is best not talked about), Sex Obsessive (sex is everything, no taboos, even young children should be conversant about it), Sex Expressive (sex is good and healthy and should be discussed appropriately).

They write:

> The aim of Sex Repressive parents is very specific: to curb sexual behavior and keep their children, especially their daughters, away from sexual entanglements before they are married. The impact of Sex Repressive parents, however, goes way beyond this goal: they instill a sense of shame in children about their innate sexuality which alienates children from their parents and interferes with their later capacity to form satisfying relationships with the opposite sex. . . .
>
> Children in these circumstances grow up feeling bad about the sexual stirrings which are an essential part of their nature, and resentful towards their parents for disapproving of this very basic aspect of their being.*

Any conscientious parent would want to be Sex Expressive, but there is for Christians a major problem with this secular view of sexuality. While it is almost always positive and healthy to be Sex Expressive, we must also instill in our children the Biblical admonition that sex before or outside of marriage is wrong, is sin, and has consequences. In other words, during the time of our children's peak sexual awareness, adolescence, we might be labeled Sex Repressive by the experts, even though we assure our children that sex is good and healthy and fun and was, in fact, God's idea.

I know some people may laugh at my notion of looking at women to appreciate God's creativity and would accuse me of inventing a spiritual reason to leer. I maintain that, after years of steeling myself to avert my eyes from something made attractive by God, developing an

---

* Miriam Ehrenberg, Ph.D., and Otto Ehrenberg, Ph.D., *The Intimate Circle* (New York: Simon and Schuster, 1988), 47–48.

appreciation for it is far healthier. Clearly it would be wrong to gawk and dwell upon some stranger's beauty, especially when I have vowed before God and man to put my wife ahead of all others. Dianna knows I am attracted to pretty women (she *is* one, after all). She also knows that I know they are off limits and that even entertaining a lustful thought is wrong. The point is, I don't pretend before my wife that I no longer look at other women. My gaze doesn't linger and my thoughts stay in check (not easily, and not always), but how much worse it would be if I pretended to have been blind since our wedding and she caught me sneaking a peek. Her standard line is, "When he quits looking, he quits cooking."

Don't get the idea that my eyes are always roving and that my poor wife can't keep my attention. (Anyone who has seen her knows otherwise.) It doesn't take a lingering look to appreciate beauty, and there are more than enough reasons not to stare at other women. First, it would threaten Dianna and jeopardize my covenant with her. It would be dangerous to my thought life, because past a casual observance of God's handiwork (go ahead, laugh!), my eyes and mind have no right to dwell there. Even if the woman doesn't belong to anyone else, I do!

It's interesting, the double standard that comes into play here. My glance at a nice looking woman is even quicker when she's escorted. I know how I feel when men stare at my wife. I watch their eyes. I'm possessive and jealous. I have a right to be. If their gaze lingers, I assume they're trying to catch her eye, and they probably are. No fair. Out of bounds. Off limits. She's mine. It gives me a great sense of security that Dianna is largely unaware how many heads she turns and that, even if she *were* aware, she's not one to return another man's gaze. Still, I resent it when I see someone stare at her, and I want to practice the golden rule when the shoe is on the other foot.

I'm quick to point out to my son that the rush of feeling he might experience for a beautiful woman should never be mistaken for true love. Such a rush is mere infatuation, physical and sensual attraction, a path to a dead end. A relationship may begin with physical attraction, but to build on that alone leads to disaster. It's also important to differentiate here between beauty and cheap sexuality. Almost any woman—within reason—can dress or make herself up in such a way that she looks sexy and available. I maintain that, unless a man is looking for thrills, he won't find such a creature attractive. Focusing on a hooker-type is selfish and fleshly, perverting the natural attraction between the sexes that was God's idea.

I realize that women may shake their heads in disgust at my obvious male perspective. Guilty. I was born this way. My friend Lois Mowday covers much the same territory from the female viewpoint in her excellent book, *The Snare*,* but neither of us could have written the other's book. Men and women think and act and are different, and no amount of modern talk can convince me otherwise.

Another high school youth leader first impressed upon me that girls don't think at all like guys do. I didn't believe him at first. Even the minor exposure to pornography a sheltered evangelical male gets tells him that women can be vamps, tramps, teases, flirts, come-ons, hookers, you name it. Therefore, the male assumes innocent, young Christian girls who dress, act, walk, or talk provocatively know exactly what they are doing. Unless

---

* See Lois Mowday, *The Snare* (Colorado Springs: Nav Press, 1988).

the girls are asking for trouble, which I find difficult to accept, they are playing a dangerous and contemptuous game with us guys. They know we are turned on by hair trigger switches through the mind and all five senses, so unless they mean business, they are cruel.

This idea that they were, on the whole, ignorant of their effect or unaware how males react was so revelatory and revolutionary that I couldn't accept it. I'm not saying there aren't women base enough to fit precisely the description in the above paragraph, but just that most of those who turn men on would be shocked to know how they are viewed.

I tested that theory as a high school senior and as a college freshman. I dated a Christian girl who was careful and virtuous and could not be described as a flirt. I discussed with her the actions and dress of mutual friends and found that she agreed with our youth leader. The girls in question were ignorant or naive. They were not sinister or on the prowl. I mustered my courage and began to ask them.

My freshman year at a Christian college allowed me to meet many beautiful women students, a whole range of personalities, modes of dress, and behavior. Our school policy stipulated that skirts could be no shorter than the top of the knee. Some of my best friends, women I respected and admired and enjoyed looking at, seemed to push the rule to the limit. How does one determine the top of the knee? (My friends and I volunteered to help!) Depending on the skirt, the material, and the woman, a skirt that was legal while she was standing might be four inches above the knee when she sat. Even the most modest skirt that touched the top of the knee was a problem for men and women when she wanted to cross her legs.

Not wanting to appear an oddball, I waited until I felt a woman was my friend before I popped my question.

"Can I ask you something, just out of curiosity?"

"Sure."

"How would you feel if you thought that the way you dressed caused men to lust?"

I asked at least six college women, ages ranging from eighteen to twenty-one. Every one of them responded with some variation on this answer:

"Oh, I'm sure we don't have any guys *that* perverted around here."

Remember, I was not on a crusade to get the rule changed or even to get the skirts lengthened. I was just testing a theory, and I was stunned by the response. They actually didn't know. They dressed for fashion, for comfort, and for their own taste. Had they realized they were causing problems for male students, I have no doubt they'd have made adjustments. In fact, things have somehow changed in the ensuing twenty years. I recently read in a Christian college newspaper an editorial by a woman student who said she and her sisters had gotten the point. They felt a responsibility not to lead their brothers into sin. She took it a step further and said some of the guys could take a lesson in how to wear their jeans.

That's a new concept: men turning women on by what they wear and how they wear it. What has contributed to this shift? Some would say novels—written by men—that portray women triggered sexually by the same stimuli that affect men, plus the advent of male strippers and magazines like *Playgirl*, which depict male nudity. It is generally accepted that women are aroused by environment, atmosphere, tenderness, romance, and touch. The idea of men baring themselves has been considered repulsive to women. Today you can even see television commercials in which girls on the beach rate the various body parts of the men that walk by. Women friends and relatives tell me, however, that while the occasional broad shoulder or narrow hip might be a mild turn-on, most women are still not sexually aroused in the same way men are. There is no longer any question that women can be aroused to a similar state of excitement and eroticism, but the route is different.*

These differences in attraction actually compete with each other. A man is turned on by the mere thought of a beautiful woman—imagining, fantasizing about the possibilities. When he meets a woman, the scenario has already been played out in his mind. She might like his voice, his smile, his manner. Meanwhile, he's light-years ahead. She smiles at his interest, then he says or does something inappropriate. Immediate disaster. She's turned off, he's offended, and neither understands what went wrong. She thinks he's a typical male. He thinks she's a typical female. Both are right. Some like to blame God for this seeming inequity ("I can't help myself; He made me this way."). Others say our makeup justifies aggressiveness, that men are to be the leaders, planners, visionaries. Women are to be submissive, supportive, reactive. Neither view is wholly acceptable, of course. Sure, there are times, especially as teen-agers, when we men might wish we hadn't been equipped with an engine that idles like a rocket but which isn't supposed to be launched for years. But to hide behind nature to justify aggression and chau-

* William H. Masters and Virginia E. Johnson, *Human Sexual Response* (Boston: Little, Brown and Company, 1966), 301–302.

vinism is cowardly. Theologians and psychologists can work out the reasons why we're made this way. Our task is to channel our drives into something positive and to glorify God in the process.

FOUR

THE DYNAMICS OF FLIRTATION

Flirting is fun and usually begins in innocence. It's a hard habit to break, even after marriage. Yet it causes jealousy. Worse, it puts us into situations we never intended to fall into, and it creates misunderstandings that can lead to infidelity.

Apart from sex, what could be more fun than flirting? If you say softball, you're reading the wrong book.

Flirting is so much fun because the rushes, emotions, and pleasures are sexual. It's foreplay with no payoff. It makes the heart race, the face flush, and a feeling of well-being wash over the body. It seems harmless, but it's not.

If you want to flirt, flirt with your wife. She may not look, feel, or sound the way she did when you first flirted with her years ago, but she still wants you to flirt with her. Try it. Wink at her across the room. Blow her a kiss no one else sees. Play footsie with her under the table. Give her a squeeze, a pinch, a tickle no one else notices.

Are you afraid she'll think you're crazy? Well, you are crazy, aren't you? Put yourself in her place. Would you like to be flirted with by someone who loves you, someone who can tease about what she might do with you later and then deliver? Do you, or would you, appreciate your wife making a pass at you, making a suggestive comment, giving you a knowing look? I do, and she does, and I love it.

Married couples do not commonly flirt with each other, and it may have to be relearned. Marital flirting is really no different than adolescent flirting. You can do the same things, only everything you're thinking about and hoping will come of it is legal, normal, acceptable, and beautiful. Marital flirting is fun and safe.

But! Who do we usually flirt with? Who would we *like* to flirt with? Good friends from work? From church? Relatives? Young people? Wives of friends?

We don't mean anything by it. It's innocent. They're safe. It's a way of having a good time at no one's expense. Right?

Then why does it bother us so much when we detect someone trying to flirt with our wives? A wink, a smile, a "Hey-why-don't-you-dump-this-guy-and-run-off-with-me-ha-ha," a touch, and the hair on our necks bristles. Who does this guy think he is? He thinks this is funny?

We're also extremely interested in how our wives react to such an approach. Can she bob and weave with the best of them, return the barbs, keep it alive? We trust her. She's faithful. It's all a game, a diversion.

Then why does it bother us so much?

Because the flirter has no right to the emotions, the inappropriate attention, the sexual/recreational lives of our spouses. I don't flirt with other women, even in jest, because I wouldn't want my wife to be offended or hurt or to wonder or be embarrassed. And I certainly would not want her to do the same.

My wife doesn't flirt because something deep within her knows it is basically wrong. She doesn't have to fight the urge, and when someone tries to flirt with her, her unpracticed reactions cool his heels. She doesn't try to be mean or cold—though she could be if someone actually came on to her—but extramarital flirtation is so far from her *modus operandi* that she usually doesn't recognize it. Thus her reaction is either puzzlement or seriousness, and a flirt needs a target that flexes, that gives, that bounces back.

Because I enjoy having fun and being funny, and because my mind tends to find humor in words and unusual combinations of ideas, I could easily flirt with anyone I thought was receptive. Much flirting is funny. If someone says something flirtatious to me, my first impulse is to expand on it, play with it, see how quick and funny I can be. But I resist that. It isn't fair. It's mental and emotional unfaithfulness. I would be exercising a portion of my brain and soul reserved for my exclusive lover.

That seems a little rigid, and I am careful not to chastise, put down, or otherwise embarrass or insult a woman who might flatter me by flirting with me. It *is* flattering, of course, even if it does somehow lower my esteem for her. I usually respond with humor that changes the subject or ends the conversation, in the hope that she will later realize that I deflected the approach without embarrassing her.

The reason I don't scowl at flirters or lecture them is that I believe most flirting is well-intentioned. It's meant to be a compliment, a friendly gesture, a you-and-me kind of a thing that separates those of us with certain kinds of minds and attitudes from everyone else in the room. It's elitist. It's subtle. It marks you as smart and clever.

But, as usual, we find ourselves confronted by the age-old difference between men and women. A friend of mine, a woman, says something grossly inappropriate to me almost every time I see her. She does it to bug me, and she has absolutely no ulterior motives. Even my wife thinks she's a scream.

Women mean something entirely different by flirting than men do. Most women I have discussed this with tell me that they agree flirting with someone else's husband is not right, and often they feel guilty later. But initiating the flirting or responding to someone's else's approach is fun and exciting because of the attention.

"Usually it surprises me," a friend says. "Often a meeting of the eyes or a smile or a flirtatious joke makes me realize for the first time that a man is even aware of me in a group. Then, I admit, I encourage it, but with no thought of actually leading him on."

I'm not saying that men intend anything serious at first either, but if a flirtatious advance is returned, it tends to escalate. I know two men who have left their wives for other men's wives, and it all began with what each party thought and intended to be harmless flirting.

In one case, the process took a year; in the other, only a little over a month. In both cases, the same thing happened. The man started it. The woman responded. They teased each other on several occasions until the man grew bold enough to think that maybe she meant something by her encouraging responses. In the first case, he made a move on her; she was stunned and hurt; and in the apologizing and reconciling process, they fell in love. In the second, she was surprised but pleased at his interest, and in the throes of a bad marriage, she jumped ship, and two marriages sank.

As with any other innocent activity that eventually gets out of hand, flirting can be a good and natural part of a person's progression toward true love. God made us able to respond emotionally and physically to attention from the opposite sex, and that is the initial aim of flirting. But like any of His gifts, this is one that can be cheapened and counterfeited and used for evil as well as for good.

I was twelve when I first experienced the euphoric surge of excitement at knowing that a girl and I had locked eyes on purpose. What began as an accident became an anticipated activity. What a revelation! It happened like this:

I helped a friend deliver papers on his route every day. We traded off, from one day to the next, handling the two halves of the territory. One day I tossed a paper onto the big front porch of a house, then moved on to the next home. I had just dropped that paper on the steps when I heard the door of the first house open and saw a girl about my age come out to retrieve the paper.

I recognized her from school, though I didn't know her—not even her name. She was probably a year ahead of me. As she bent to pick up the paper, her long brown hair cascaded over her face, and as she stood up, she flipped it back into place with a turn of her head. And she looked right at me.

I had been idly watching her as I moved along, but I was embarrassed that she saw me, so I quickly looked elsewhere. But what was that out of the corner of my eye?

Had I turned too quickly? Had she smiled at me? I shot a fast double take her way; she had already turned back toward the door. But out of the corner of her eye she must have seen me looking back at her, so she turned back.

We smiled shyly at each other and said nothing. I don't know what she was thinking. Probably nothing. To a twelve-year-old, a thirteen-year-old is almost an adult, and I was very much on the young side of twelve. I probably had a ball glove in my newspaper bag, maybe even a pocketful of marbles. My hair would have been flying.

She was more sophisticated. Grown up. She was probably just smiling at some dumb paperboy, I decided, but I sure liked it when she smiled at me. The next day I pleaded with my friend to let me deliver on the same end of the route again. Nothing doing. I would have to wait another twenty-four hours to see that smile. I never considered that it was probably a fluke. Why hadn't I ever seen her before? Did I think she would wait at the window for me next time?

Two days later my hair was combed, my cleanest jeans were on, and I wore new tennies. I imagined her watching me from half way down the block, so I did my best to look older, more conscientious, important, in a hurry, doing a good job. A couple of times I walked past a house without dropping a paper, only to nonchalantly flip one behind my back to the precise spot. I was hot.

At the house before hers I had to mount the steps and put the paper in the rungs under the mail box. I casually bounded up the stairs two at a time, slipped the paper in, and jumped all the way to the ground. No problem. I don't know what I would have done if I had wound up with a face full of dirt. I never thought about that. I imagined her eyes on me, smiling, and I could do anything. Down deep I was hoping against hope that she was home and would come out to get the paper again.

I approached her porch. Slowly. Dropped the paper in front of the door. Turned. More slowly. Then moved resolutely to the next house. No action. No movement. No noise. I looked back several times, hoping. Nothing. Maybe that's why I was doing only one side of the street at a time. When I crossed at the corner and delivered papers to the other side of the same street, I could see her porch for half a block. I worked ever so deliberately.

The house directly across from hers was not that of a paper subscriber, but it sat on a wide expanse of lawn. I delivered the paper to the house before it, then traversed the entire distance to the next subscriber with my head turned, staring at the magic porch. Had someone planted a tree in my path the day before, I'd have worn it home. The trail I blazed was as circuitous as you can imagine for one without his eye on where he's going.

But my persistence paid off. She appeared. And she was dressed up in a fluffy, red dress. She stepped out, picked up the paper, went to the edge of the porch, leaned on the railing, and smiled at me across the street. Her smile and her eyes followed me until I had to look away or careen into the street. This had been no accident. I couldn't swear she had dressed up just for me—clearly she had somewhere to go early that evening—but she had looked for me, found me, smiled at me, and made it obvious she was pleased to have done so. I began wondering where we might raise our family.

You can't imagine the thrill, unless you remember similar experiences on the threshold of puberty. We continued that ritual every other day for a little over a week, until I found out she was doing the same to my friend, the other delivery boy. I hadn't even said hello to my intended, and she had already cheated on me. I wasn't even motivated to fight for her. My interest cooled overnight.

As a freshman in high school I enjoyed another silent flirting season with a girl in my algebra class. She was a fresh-faced blond with glasses and a turned-up nose, and for some reason, I loved to look at her. We sat on opposite sides of the room. To see her, I had to lean back and look past all the heads in my row. One day she caught me looking, so I turned back. But when I sneaked another peek, she was staring right at me.

It seemed my heart skipped a beat. Was it obvious to everyone in the class that we were in love? I didn't even know her name, yet my pulse quickened and I was short of breath when I caught her gaze, me leaning back and her leaning forward. We didn't even smile at each other. This was too intense. Occasionally I tried to tell myself I was imagining this, and then we would settle into our desks, the teacher would begin his lecture, and I would zero in on that pair of eyes.

For a week we stared at each other, sometimes for twenty minutes at a time. I was stunned the teacher did not call us down for it, or at least one of us. He would not have been able to see both of us staring at the same time, but he could have followed one's gaze to the other. Either he didn't notice or he had already given up on my algebra potential.

One day, when I had finally learned her name, I mustered the courage to send a note across to her. Everybody looked at her and then at me as she read it. "See you after class?" it read. She looked up at me, still unsmiling, and nodded. Has there ever been a longer forty-minute wait? I couldn't even look at her that day. I just studied the clock.

After class she went out the door, turned right, stood with her back against the wall and her books embraced in front of her and waited expectantly. "Hi," I said.

"Hi," she said.

I wanted so badly to say something cool like, "You know, I've really enjoyed studying you these last several days, and I thought it was time we got better acquainted."

But I didn't. I said, "Um, I was wonderin' if you wouldn't mind if I walked you to your next class."

"No problem," she said, in a voice too hard, too sharp for such a pretty face. "'Cept it's like right here." She nodded to the study hall next to the algebra room.

"Oh, yeah, well, I guess you can make it there by yourself all right."

"Yeah," she said, and walked away.

I saw her again, but I never looked at her, if you know what I mean. I was learning valuable lessons in illusion versus reality.

My point in these two anecdotes, however, is that the same surge of ecstasy is available to me—or to any man—today. If you work at it, you can catch a woman's eye and see if she wants to play the game. The problem is that it's short of adultery only in the physical sense, and it can lead to that.

I'm sometimes embarrassed in public, maybe in a restaurant, when I happen to catch the gaze of a woman, look away, and then we look back at the same moment. Neither of us is looking for anything; each is embarrassed and wonders what the other thinks. I usually smile apologetically and then fight the urge to look once more.

I'm not looking for other women's eyes, and I don't want them or anyone, especially my wife, to think that I am. There is a comfort, a sensuality, a sexuality, a bonding deeper than with anyone else when I look deeply into Dianna's eyes. I know her, I can read her, and we can communicate that way.

I also communicate with her by flirting, touching, caressing, yes, even playing footsie. We consider these fun and funny ways of communicating to be personal and private. They make up a part of our sexual language of love, and every one of them — even the looks, smiles, and suggestive comments — are off limits for anyone else.

I don't flirt with anyone but my wife, and vice-versa.

FIVE

THE BIBLICAL BASIS FOR HEDGES

People will tell you to beware of legalism, even in the area of sexual purity. It's true that a balanced, appropriate view makes our stand attractive rather than shrill, but Scripture is clear. There's a price to pay.

We're far enough along in this book now that the following should be no revelation: I am making the assumption that you care what God thinks about your life. If you don't care, you're reading the wrong book. I believe in God, and I accept the Bible as the basis of authority for my life. If you don't, this has all long since appeared foolish to you anyway.

Perhaps you're in the middle on these issues. Maybe you aren't sure about a personal God and are *very* unsure whether the Bible is relevant. That puts you in the same category, sadly, as many who call themselves Christians. They are smorgasbord church people who sample what looks good to them and leave what doesn't. And a God who cares about our sexual conduct and even has rules regarding it doesn't seem to fit our contemporary, "me-first" society.

The problem with that view is that it assumes God has rules for rules' sake. He's just a spoil sport, trying to make a goody-two-shoes out of everybody. If we can't find practical reasons for following His rules, we justify ignoring them.

My simple mind cries out for a God who is personal, orderly, and logical. I believe that a God who created everything and loved us enough to make the supreme sacrifice for us has reasons for His prohibitions and would rather see us happy and fulfilled than miserable and confined.

If I'm right, there must be sense and logic behind His rules. Let's look at them briefly to determine what they are, and then let me make an amateur's—or at least a layman's—attempt at making them fit with my view of God as a fulfiller, not a taskmaster.

Here Comes the Judge

Jesus talks about the law most extensively in Matthew 5:17–19:

> Do not think that I came to destroy the Law or the Prophets. I did not come to destroy but to fulfill. For assuredly, I say to you, till heaven and earth pass away, one jot or one tittle will by no means pass from the law till all is fulfilled. Whoever therefore breaks one of the least of these commandments, and teaches men so, shall be called least in the kingdom of heaven; but whoever does and teaches them, he shall be called great in the kingdom of heaven.

The law He's talking about, of course, is the Ten Commandments. Most people, even non-churchgoers, can remember a few of them. Don't lie, don't murder, don't commit adultery, don't steal. We can see the obvious problems with lying, stealing, and murdering, but if sex is so good and beautiful and fun, what's wrong with a little adultery among friends?

And what is Jesus talking about when He says He's fulfilling, not replacing, the law? This is the wrong forum from which to get into Jesus' claims of deity, but suffice it to say He was establishing Himself as one with God, the Son of God, the fulfillment of God's law. The embodiment of perfection, the personification of sinlessness, was Jesus Christ. Now, lest anyone else claim to also qualify as the righteous king, Jesus, in essence, changes all the rules.

Later in the same discourse He says,

> Unless your righteousness exceeds the righteousness of the scribes and Pharisees, you will by no means enter the kingdom of heaven.
>
> You have heard that it was said to those of old, "You shall not murder," and whoever murders will be in danger of the judgment. But I say to you that whoever is angry with his brother without a cause shall be in danger of the judgment. (Matthew 5:20–22)

Murder is worthy of judgment, but now even anger with a brother is just as bad! Who can live up to that standard? Only Jesus. Then He gets down to the toughest part. "You have heard that it was said to those of old, 'You shall not commit adultery.' But I say to you that whoever looks at a woman to lust for her has already committed adultery with her in his heart" (Matthew 5:27, 28).

What is the point of all that? Wasn't the original law hard enough? Wasn't it a good enough standard by which to be judged? Why would Jesus rewrite it and make it impossible? Let me speculate, as a layman. Jesus, the God/Man who died for us, could take no pleasure in making life difficult or unachievable for us. Clearly He was setting a standard here to make a point. The point was that if someone was somehow able to keep from lying, murdering, even coveting for an entire lifetime, there was no way to ever dream of following this *new* standard. Hatred, anger, is murder. Lust is adultery. We're all guilty.

Only Jesus could meet and fulfill that standard, so we are forced to rely upon Him for our standing before God. He takes the penalty for our sin; He becomes our advocate before Holy God. God looks at us and sees not our sin but the perfection of Jesus, and we who would otherwise be unqualified to be in His presence are assured of a place with Him for eternity. The apostle Paul said it this way in 2 Corinthians 5:21: "For He made Him who knew no sin to be sin for us, that we might become the righteousness of God in Him."

Between Our Ears

When my friend Robert Wolgemuth teaches from Matthew, he makes the point that what Jesus was really talking about was not murder or adultery but attitudes, what goes on between our ears. He's talking about the things most people can't see. Jesus is saying that the law is not something you do or don't do; it's something you are.

The question then arises as to why Jesus puts adultery in the same category as murder. Leviticus 20:10 says, "The man who commits adultery with another man's wife, he who commits adultery with his neighbor's wife, the adulterer and the adulteress, shall surely be put to death." Murderers and adulterers deserve death, according to the law, and Jesus has made the law impossible to obey. What's going on?

A lot of this, I admit, will not be comprehensible this side of heaven, but we had better find out why these two sins are considered equally reprehensible before we start building our lives on our own principles. Why was it so important that people not commit adultery? I submit that the reasons, whatever they are, are the same reasons we need to build hedges around our hearts, eyes, hands, spouses, and marriages. If adultery is in the same class as murder, it is a threat not only to our marriages but to our very lives.

Some have said that only a crazy person can commit murder. A man or woman has to lose contact with reality to become so angry or distraught or jealous that he or she can take another's life. I've found that adulterers suffer from this same malady. They'll violate a vow they made years before, drag their wife and family through torture and disgrace, and set aside or reformat their entire set of values. How else could a man justify the chaos wrought by his actions?

A friend of mine once found himself pulled into a situation in which he was to officiate at a family meeting where an adulterous father tried to explain to his children, in front of his wife, why he was leaving her for another woman. One of this man's first assertions was that he had never really loved his wife. (To a person who believes that love is a feeling rather than an act of the will, falling out of love or deciding you never loved someone is a convenient rationalization.)

The young teen son admitted to his father that he didn't understand. "How, after all these years, can you say you don't love Mom? After all we've done together . . ."

The only way the man could live with himself was to tell himself lies, to reorder his standards. He asked his younger daughter, "Honey, tell me what you're thinking."

She looked up at him, fighting for composure. "I'm thinking I'm sad," she said.

Adultery Causes Chaos

Adulterers are liars, and they are as good at it as alcoholics are. Another friend of mine was awakened in the middle of the night by a call informing him of the infidelity of a good buddy. He didn't believe it, so he went to see his buddy. "Dave," he said, "what's the story about you and this woman?"

Dave played dumb. "It's not true," he said, looking my friend squarely in the eye. "No way. Not me. Never have, never will."

"Wait a minute," my friend said. "What about all these allegations?" He proceeded with a litany of charges, names, dates, places.

"Someone's trying to frame me," Dave said. "Never happened."

What a relief! My friend wouldn't have to see this man confess to his wife, disappointing her, breaking her heart, ruining their marriage. It was good news.

Good news until two months later, when my friend's wife got a call from Dave's wife. She was frantic, nearly hysterical. My friend and his wife raced to her home while Dave was away on business. She had discovered the affair and had a pile of evidence to prove it. My friend was assigned to meet Dave at the airport upon his return. Rather than being met by his family as usual, Dave was puzzled to see my friend standing there solemnly. "It's over," my friend told him. "Your wife knows and I know."

He led him out to the parking lot where his car was jammed floor to ceiling with his belongings. There was barely room for the two men. Dave drove my friend home and then set out to look for a place to live. My friend watched him pull out of sight in the darkness and he knew: Adultery causes chaos.

I had an acquaintance once tell me that yes, he had been seeing another woman, but that no, he was not interested in her romantically and didn't think she was interested in him either. They were just friends. Middle of the night, sometimes all night friends. He liked her baby daughter. Yeah, that was it. They had a lot in common, talked easily, liked each other's company. I told him he didn't have the right to have a woman as a close friend when he was married and that it was slowly killing his wife.

He seemed to see the light, said he would break it off that night, and I returned to his wife with the wonderful news. That night he met the woman after work. I saw them embrace and kiss before they left the state in her car. By the time he really came to his senses and pleaded for his wife to take him back—he missed his four boys terribly—the divorce was final.

Adultery causes chaos.

Are You Guilty?

As much as television, movies, and videos try to convince us otherwise, adultery is not funny. The media has convinced too many people that adultery is no more serious than exceeding the speed limit. Everybody does it. This is a new age. Don't be so old-fashioned. Get with the program!

If the Bible deals with this modern issue, it had better do it in a sophisticated, up-to-date way or no one will pay any attention. What could a musty old religious tome have to say about life as we know it today?

Remember Leviticus 20:10? Adulterers are put to death. Remember Matthew 5:27, 28? Lust is adultery. Are you guilty? You may be guilty of more than lust. You may be guilty of adultery itself, and more than once. Be glad Jesus fulfilled the law for you, because even if your offense was the attitude and not the act, you were still guilty.

There is forgiveness. There is starting over. There is a future for you. John 8:3–11 tells this story:

> Then the scribes and Pharisees brought to Him a woman caught in adultery. And when they had set her in the midst, they said to Him, "Teacher, this woman was caught in adultery, in the very act. Now Moses, in the law, commanded us that such should be stoned. But what do You say?" This they said, testing Him, that they might have something of which to accuse Him.
>
> But Jesus stooped down and wrote on the ground with His finger, as though He did not hear. So when they continued asking Him, He raised Himself up and said to them, "He who is without sin among you, let him throw a stone at her first." And again He stooped down and wrote on the ground.
>
> Then those who heard it, being convicted by their conscience, went out one by one, beginning with the oldest even to the last. And Jesus was left alone, and the woman standing in the midst.

> When Jesus had raised Himself up and saw no one but the woman, He said to her, "Woman, where are those accusers of yours? Has no one condemned you?"
>
> She said, "No one, Lord."
>
> And Jesus said to her, "Neither do I condemn you; go and sin no more."

Don't make the mistake of assuming Jesus was condoning adultery. He called her adultery sin and told her to sin no more. I've always appreciated the irony in this story. Jesus says that the one "among you" without sin should cast the first stone. Have you ever thought about the fact that there *was* one among them who was without sin? It was Jesus Himself. And He chose not to cast a stone.

His point was to label the accusers as adulterers, because indeed we all are—even if we have never committed the act. We may not have murdered, but we have hated; and we may not have committed adultery, but we have lusted. And Jesus says to us with the voice of loving forgiveness that rings through the ages: "Neither do I condemn you; go and sin no more."

Out of pure thanks and appreciation and wonder at that freeing compassion, we should want to obey.

But What About Temptation?

First Corinthians 10:13 says, "No temptation has overtaken you except such as is common to man; but God is faithful, who will not allow you to be tempted beyond what you are able, but with the temptation will also make the way of escape, that you may be able to bear it."

The problem with lust and its result is that it is difficult to resist and that people try everything to win over it.

They pray, they stand and fight, they resolve, when all the while our plan of attack is clear—and it's not a plan of attack at all. We are to retreat! Paul wrote to his young friend in 2 Timothy 2:22: "Flee also youthful lusts; but pursue righteousness, faith, love, peace with those who call on the Lord out of a pure heart."

The problem with the temptation verse (1 Corinthians 10:13) is that people apply it too late. Ten minutes into foreplay with the wrong partner, they're ready to seek that way of escape that was supposed to have come with the temptation. That's just it: The escape comes *with* the temptation. It's preventive medicine, not first-aid after you've already set your course on a path toward injury.

More Biblical Bases for Hedges

Need any more evidence that there are biblical bases for planting hedges around your marriage? Psalm 89:40 implies that strongholds are brought to ruin when hedges are broken down. Job 1:10 implies that Job was so richly blessed—before God allowed him to be tested—because God had made a hedge around him, his household, "and around all that he has on every side."

Jesus told parables about landowners who planted vineyards and protected them with hedges. When those hedges were trampled or removed, ruin came to the precious possessions of the landowners.

We hold people and relationships much more precious than land or holdings. If we can keep from deceiving ourselves about our own resolve and inner strength, we will see the necessity for a healthy row of blossoming hedges that keep love in and infidelity out.

SIX

THE POWER OF SELF-DECEPTION

Knowing our own weaknesses is one way to begin tilling the soil for the seeds of the hedges that will protect us.

Before I get into my own list of hedges, which evidences also my own weaknesses, I need to ask you: what are yours?

A friend of mine has planted two hedges for his business life. First, he stays away from pornography, which is becoming more difficult all the time. Rather than pretend to be disgusted and turned off by it, he admits it can be seductive. It can be tantalizing. Although looking at pornography may result in his feeling disgusted with himself and wondering how he could ever be attracted to such a cheapening of God's gift of sexuality, he is more successful in fending it off by acknowledging *in advance* that it's something he wants to avoid. So, if it's pumped into his hotel room via television, he tells the front desk to lock it out. Sometimes the clerk will act surprised or wonder aloud if he has children with him in spite of his reservation as a single. My friend doesn't let this daunt him. He clarifies he is alone and insists on the lock-out service. As part of this hedge he often travels with his business partner, and they keep each other honest.

What if my friend told himself that since he had gone many years without succumbing to the temptation of pornography, he could surely travel on his own and not have to embarrass himself by asking a desk clerk half his age to lock out the adult movies? A sexy show on regular television might whet his appetite for something racier, something he might not even consider if he did not know it was available. But with the seemingly innocuous touch of a button, with the first five minutes not even billed to his room, he might convince himself he's mature enough to satisfy his curiosity.

The key is preventive maintenance. Once that first step has been taken down the road of self-deceit and rationalization, there is no turning back. Each excuse sounds more plausible, and before he knows it, the typical male has satisfied every curiosity, every urge. Regardless of the remorse, the self-loathing, and the pledges for the future, the pattern will repeat itself for as long as he refuses to flee. There is no other defense.

My friend's second hedge comes in the form of pictures he carries in his wallet of his wife and his two daughters. These pictures serve the usual function of reminding him of his loved ones and allowing him to brag about his beautiful family. But they also serve as a safety net, which he used several years ago when he found himself next to a beautiful, young, single woman on an airplane.

Normally he feigns fatigue and isn't interested in conversing during a long flight, but this woman was fun to look at and more fun to talk to. He asked her about herself. She sounded more interesting and exciting every minute. She was staying in the same city for which he was headed. She had a car and could give him a ride to his hotel. And why not? Each seemed nice enough to the other.

We're Not All the Same

To illustrate differences in styles and personalities, I must say that I would have hid behind a hedge I planted years ago that does not allow me to accept a ride alone with an unrelated woman. I wouldn't trust my weak, self-deceiving, rationalizing mind once I was alone with a beautiful, willing female. My friend, however, used a different hedge and was able to accept the ride. When she asked about him, he pulled out his wallet. Before he showed her the photos of his wife and daughters, he looked at them himself.

"It was as if they spoke to me right out of that wallet," he says. "They said, 'Thanks, Daddy, for being faithful to Mom and to us.'"

He smiled as he showed her the pictures and spoke lovingly of his family, especially of his wife, Jackie. The conversation mellowed and became friendly in a different sort of way than before. My friend rode with the woman to his hotel, shook her hand, and heard her say in farewell, "Say hi to Jackie for me."

"If you think I didn't want to spend the night with her," he admits, "you're crazy."

But it sure wasn't worth his spiritual, mental, and family life. He used a hedge, one that wouldn't have worked for me, but an effective one for him and his personality.

Custom-make Your Hedges

Just as my friend used a different hedge than I would have, so there are also temptations difficult for some and not for others. For instance, the temptation to frequent prostitutes happens to be one I can only write about and not identify with. I know it's a very real temptation and that it has been the ruin "of many a poor boy." I know this temptation is one that has been the ruin of Christians, even preachers, and that the book of Proverbs is replete with admonition about and against it. It just happens, though, that this is an area in which I have never been tempted—although I was propositioned once.

I was on business in Cleveland and had innocently booked a hotel room in the seediest part of town. The hotel chain was a large, well-known one, so I was stunned when I went out for a walk and found myself in the red light district. While I might have been young and curious enough to be tempted to slip into an adult movie theater, my fear of a fire bomb or a raid was sufficient defense. "Christian Writer Among Dead in Adult Theater Fire" would have been a nice final page for my wife's scrapbook, huh? I know that fear of detection is not the highest motive for avoiding such temptations, but you tend to use whatever works at the point of weakness and develop the proper spiritual discipline and reasoning later.

It was dark out and the area seemed overrun with potential muggers. I was hurrying back to my hotel when a teen-aged hooker made me an offer I'm sure she thought I couldn't refuse. I was nearly paralyzed. I had always wondered what I would say. This girl was not unattractive, but I had not the slightest second thought. The question was what I would say.

I could have ignored her and kept walking, which is what I would do today. I could have looked shocked and disgusted and told her off. I could have witnessed to her. (I have friends who do that, but I don't recommend it unless you're with your wife or a group. Say the wrong thing while witnessing to an undercover cop and you'll find yourself, and your ministry, in the overnight lock-up. Or, if you're alone, try explaining to someone who recognizes you just what you were saying to the hooker on the corner.)

Well, I was in my early twenties, and all my upbringing and training came to the fore. I was polite, maddeningly, and as I think about it, hilariously polite. I said, "No, thanks."

She acted disappointed and asked, "Are you sure?"

"Yes, but thanks, anyway."

"Whatcha wanna be alone for tonight when you can be indulgin' yourself?"

"That's all right," I said. "I hope you won't be offended if I pass."

As she shrugged and trudged on, I thought, *I hope you won't be offended! What a stupid thing to say!* That girl was threatening my moral and spiritual health, trying to get me to jeopardize my marriage, encouraging me to go against everything I had ever been taught or believed, and I was polite!

Are You Lonesome Tonight?

I was with an older colleague in a top flight hotel in Detroit several years ago when we smelled perfume and heard a spraying sound near the door. He tiptoed over in stocking feet to discover that indeed someone was spraying perfume under the door. He swung the door open to see a middle-aged woman in a mini-skirt leaning seductively in the frame.

"You lonely, Hon?" she asked.

"I'll never be that lonely," he said, and shut the door. I wish I'd thought of that.

On the other hand, I heard a prominent preacher say that he got on an elevator in a hotel in a big city and was greeted warmly by two beautiful young women. A glib, social type, he engaged them in friendly banter for a few seconds before they boldly asked him to join them in their room. "In the space of less than a minute, I had to make a decision," he says. "I was far from home. I could get away with this, in one sense." He knew it would be wrong, silently prayed for the strength to resist, and left the elevator on his own floor.

I know it can be disappointing to hear that a man of God would even have to talk himself out of something like that, but each man carries with him his own weaknesses and temptations. Whereas I have never been able even to imagine being attracted to or turned on by a woman who has had sex with others all day, I need to plant hedges against being alone or working too closely with women I simply admire or like. That, to me, is more dangerous. I could see myself becoming attached to or enamored with someone I worked with if I didn't emphasize keeping everything on a professional basis.

A Word of Caution

Just because I cannot imagine ever being tempted by a prostitute doesn't mean I am cavalier or naive about their areas and haunts. There are other forms of illegal activity that don't tempt me either, but I don't hang around their headquarters.

In other words, if you're tempted to cruise prostitution row, the way of escape is to do something else. Go somewhere else. While you have your wits about you—before you're at the edge of the abyss—make a rule for yourself that you won't drive within a certain number of blocks of the area for any reason.

Some hedges may appear ridiculous to you because they are unnecessary in your life—just like the one above is for me. I used to drive home right through an area where hookers frequented the corners. I knew enough not to look interested, because I truly wasn't. I was curious, sure, wondering about these sad girls with wasted bodies and faces, clearly addicted to drugs, waving at cars and trying to avoid detection by police. But tempting it was not.

A man I used to work with told me he drove through that area and that as he was looking at a hooker while at a stoplight, she approached his car. She asked if he wanted a date. He said no, but she seemed friendly and so he asked her what the going rate was for a date. She told him, he smiled at her, waved, and drove off. I knew him. He would not have been any more attracted to a prostitute than I was, but he had been stupid. Somehow, even with the spate documentaries and dramas about the world of prostitution, he had missed the fact that negotiating the price is the operative offense that can get you locked up. Had his hooker been an undercover cop, he would have been arrested for negotiating with a prostitute.

Stupidity

Too many men are stupid in other ways. They think they can handle any temptation. Their resolve, their marriage, their spirituality will carry the day. These men are self-deceived, and we all know too many of them.

No one wants to admit he has a problem or a weakness. I confess it bothered me when I heard the minister in the hotel elevator story above give that account. I wondered why he didn't admit to some other, less offensive temptation, like maybe the urge to spend more on a car than he should have. For some reason we don't want our spiritual heroes to be human. Wives don't want their husbands to be human. Kids don't want their dads to be human. We'd all like to know someone who is so spiritual, so wise, so disciplined that he could ignore or throw away a men's magazine left in his hotel room by the previous guest. I'll tell you, if I didn't throw it out upon first discovering it, ignoring it would be a chore.

No one likes to admit that. I can hear people saying, "How disgusting! Who would want to poison his mind with that trash?"

Certainly not I. Or would I? All I know to do, according to Paul's letter to Timothy, is to flee. Why? Because of what Paul also says in his letter to the Romans:

> For what I am doing, I do not understand. For what I will to do, that I do not practice; but what I hate, that I do. If, then, I do what I will not to do, I agree with the law that it is good. But now, it is no longer I who do it, but sin that dwells in me. For I know that in me (that is, in my flesh) nothing good dwells; for to will is present with me, but how to perform what is good I do not find. (Romans 7:15–18)

And in Romans 7:22–25:

> For I delight in the law of God according to the inward man. But I see another law in my members, warring against the law of my mind, and bringing me into captivity to the law of sin which is in my members. O wretched man that I am! Who will deliver me from this body of death? I thank God—through Jesus Christ our Lord! So then, with the mind I myself serve the law of God, but with the flesh the law of sin.

The only future in self-deceit is ruin. Let's quit kidding ourselves. No, we don't have to broadcast every base thought and urge to the public, but in our heart of hearts, let's avoid denial. If the greatest missionary in the history of Christendom could make himself vulnerable by admitting that in his flesh dwells no good thing, who are we to think we should be above carnal drives and desires?

The only regret I have since going on my hedges campaign a few years ago is that occasionally some wonderful woman colleague or new friend will say, "I don't know how to act around you, whether I can touch you or not, or just shake your hand."

The last thing I want is a reputation as a guy who is desperately trying to contain his lustful thoughts for everything in a skirt. As you'll see later, I do trust myself to touch and even embrace women I'm not related to. But I have strict guidelines and hedges, because I do not want to fall to my own self-deceit.

Let's start planting some practical hedges.

PART TWO

HOW TO START PLANTING

Here are pragmatic ways to guard ourselves against our weaknesses. We can plant hedges only after we have determined where they must grow.

SEVEN

TWO'S COMPANY; THREE'S SECURITY

Hedge No. 1—Whenever I need to meet or dine or travel with an unrelated woman, I make it a threesome. Should an unavoidable last-minute complication make this impossible, my wife hears it from me first.

This hedge is about pure logic. Scripture is clear that Christians should "abstain from sexual immorality" (1 Thessalonians 4:3), for "this is the will of God."

So, you ask, what is sexually immoral about meeting, dining, or traveling with an unrelated woman? Nothing. But it is also true that, unless I am alone with a woman, I will not engage in immorality.

But, you're still wondering, what does one necessarily have to do with the other? In other words, if it is true that I won't commit adultery if I'm not alone with a woman, is it also true that if I am alone with her, I will? No, that is not logical. Logic says that if I am also following the Biblical injunction to abstain from even the appearance of evil (1 Thessalonians 5:22), I will also abstain from the evil itself.

My philosophy is, if you take care of how things look, you take care of how they are.

Where I work we have a tiny window in every office door. When these were installed forty or fifty years ago, they were not intended to make immorality difficult. They were intended to eliminate suspicion and protect reputations. As long as that little eye to the outside world is uncovered, no one feels free to attempt anything untoward, and just as importantly, no one else is suspicious about what goes on behind closed doors. Were it not for those little windows, I would feel obligated to invite my secretary to every brief meeting I might have with a woman, or to keep my door open.

Why? Am I really that weak or dangerous? Or are those with whom I might meet? No, I don't think so. But I don't want the reputations of the woman, my employer, my wife, or my Lord—not to mention myself—even to be questioned.

Risky Business

One of the saddest and scariest stories I've ever heard on this subject was about a young evangelist. He was just barely twenty-one, on fire for God, effective in his preaching and soul-winning, and in great demand from local churches. He had preached several large crusades and was soon invited to an area-wide effort at which he would be the main speaker.

Though he was not yet even out of college, he was a protégé of international evangelist, Sammy Tippit, and was admired and considered wise. Though he didn't have a steady girlfriend, he dated regularly at Bible college. Spiritually he was alert and mature. He was, however, naive. The first night of the crusade he headed up the counseling ministry in a large room near the pastor's study. A beautiful teen-ager asked if she could speak with him personally. He tried to assign her to someone else, but when she persisted, he agreed for her to wait until he was finished with the others.

More than an hour after the meeting had ended, the rest of the counselors and counselees had left, and he was alone with the young girl. A few minutes later she burst from the room, screaming, "He made a pass at me! He wanted to make love to me!"

That very night the pastor of the host church and a small group of the crusade planners confronted the young preacher and demanded an explanation. He denied the girl's charge but had no witnesses. The girl had seemed an upstanding young woman in the church, and there was no reason to disbelieve her story.

"What did happen in that room?" the pastor demanded.

"To tell you that would be to make an accusation behind someone's back," he said. "Which is what happened to me. I ask only that I be allowed to face my accuser." The pastor and the others canceled the rest of the crusade and agreed that the young woman should be asked to face the preacher in their presence. Two nights later she showed up with her parents at a private board meeting. The pastor asked if she would care to speak about her charges against the preacher.

"She has already said all she has to say," her father said sternly, her mother nodding and glaring at the accused.

"Would you, son, care to share your version of what happened in that room the other night?"

"No, sir," the evangelist said. "I see no future in that. Only she and I know the truth, and I cannot defend myself. I'd just like to say this to her. Cindy, you know what happened and what didn't happen in that room. If you don't tell the truth, I will be branded and may never preach again. This will damage my reputation and that of this church and even that of God. If I did what you say I did, I deserve no better, but we both know that is not the truth. I'm begging you in the name of Christ to set the record straight."

The silence hung heavy as the board and her parents watched her face contort into a grimace before the tears began to flow. "I lied," she said quietly. "I'm sorry. I lied. He didn't make a pass at me; I made a pass at him. When he turned me down I was so embarrassed and ashamed and angry that I made up that story. I'm so sorry!"

Had that young evangelist not had the wisdom to face his accuser in just that manner, his ministry might have been ruined forever. And had not God worked in that young girl's heart, she might have sat there silently, refusing to change her story.

That preacher is no longer young. He has never again allowed himself to be alone in a room with a female to whom he is not related. Along with his spiritual wisdom came a painful, almost fatal, farewell to naiveté. He might have been embarrassed that night, early in his ministry, if he'd had to ask someone to stay with him while he counseled the young woman, or if he'd had to tell her that he could see her only in the sanctuary. But now he sees embarrassment, or sometimes even the risk of offending, a small price to pay for the protection of all those reputations.

A Movable Feast

You may have noticed that I included dining alone with my meeting and traveling prohibitions. I don't know why, but there is something very personal and even intimate about eating with someone. If that weren't true, why are so many dates centered on food?

My embargo against dining alone with an unrelated woman is also for my wife's sake. Dianna is not the jealous type, but this way I don't have to keep track of every lunch partner so I can tell her about each one before someone else does. People love to say, "Oh, I saw your husband having lunch with so-and-so the other day," with that lilt in their voice that begs to know if anything is going on.

My intention is that if someone told Dianna that I had been seen with someone alone, she would immediately say, "No, he wasn't," because she knows if that were to happen, she would have known about it first. Once my secretary and I invited a friend of hers to have lunch with us. At the last minute the friend was unable to go. We just changed our plans, had the lunch delivered, and enjoyed it in the office with the door open. I mentioned it to my wife in advance, just as a courtesy.

The first few times my secretary and I changed our plans because a third party was unavailable, she may have thought I was being a bit ridiculous. She had no designs on me, and vice versa, though we are friends. I'm sure I seemed to be straining at a gnat. But over the years, as we have seen marriage after marriage fail and family after family suffer, my prudish rules seem to have made more sense.

There will always be times, of course, when rules cannot be followed to the letter. During the years when I was headquartered ten miles north of our campus, I occasionally found it necessary to drop a woman off at one location or another. Sometimes this came up when it was inconvenient or impossible to let my wife know in advance. It would have been silly to wait until I could either tell her or appear to ask permission. I told her later and, though she never demanded it, she always appreciated it. On those rare occasions when I do question the reputation of one with whom I might have to meet or dine or travel alone, I don't think twice. I don't call to inform Dianna or to ask her permission. I just don't go.

On the Road

Travel is chock full of dangerous possibilities for appearances and behavior. Assume that every motive is pure. How does it look for a man and a woman who don't belong to each other to be on a long trip together, in a car, on a plane, in a cab, at the same hotel—even if in separate rooms?

I had to travel to a distant city with a woman manager who reported to me, so I asked her to select someone to go with us. The young woman she chose woke up ill on departure day, and I didn't learn about it until I arrived at the airport. My manager was also a friend of our family, which helped, and though she was single and close to my age, our relationship was such that we didn't worry about anything happening. We worried most about how the trip would look.

Because originally she had planned to room with the younger woman, we had thought nothing of booking our seats together on the plane and sharing a ride to—and staying at—the same hotel. All those arrangements had been made, but I was willing to absorb the cost of canceling them if necessary. My first query was to the manager herself. She expressed her knowledge of, trust in, and respect for me; and said she had no problem traveling with me, but that she would understand if I chose not to go.

I then called my boss. An unwritten rule in our ministry forbids unrelated men and women traveling together without a third party, but under the circumstances my boss left it up to me. With a phone call from the airport, I passed the buck to my wife. She nearly laughed. The fact that I had called her and had made a practice of keeping her informed of such seeming improprieties for years gave her the confidence to immediately agree.

Advice from One Who Knows

In the July 1985 issue of *Advance* magazine,* evangelist Robert M. Abbott writes that, just as the fact that "a certain percentage of people die annually through traffic accidents does not mean we stop searching for ways to

---

* Robert M. Abbott, "Thank God for Brakes," *Advance,* (July 1985).

remedy the situation," neither should we be ready to shrug off moral impurity among our leaders.

Abbott continues, "None of us plan[s] to have moral accidents, but we must also plan *not* to! Danger rides with us all the time." He compares the moral danger to that of a driver pulling several tons of equipment behind his car. "[This] requires more braking power and a longer stopping time . . . Brakes! Thank God for brakes!"

Abbott writes that "[we] must learn to keep plenty of space between us and sinful acts, so we can start braking soon enough to stop before it is too late." He offers a list of twenty-eight times when we might "need to put on the brakes early and well." Among them:

- When you are so busy there is no time to be alone with God.
- When you are too busy to spend at least one relaxed evening a week with your wife and family.
- When you feel you deserve more attention than you are getting at home.
- When you wouldn't want your wife [or a colleague] to see what you are reading or looking at.
- When the romance in your marriage is fading.
- When your charisma, appearance, and personality are attractive to women, and you are tempted to make the most of it.
- When you enjoy fantasizing about an illicit relationship.
- When a woman makes herself available by her behavior.

- When some woman tells you how wonderful you are and how much she loves you.
- When Scriptures concerning adultery are for others, not you.
- When you start feeling sorry for yourself.
- When you hope God isn't looking or listening.

Sadly, so many pastors and other Christian leaders fall into sexual temptation because of a common problem. They have planted no hedges and find themselves counseling weeping, exasperated women who seem to have a lot to offer but are frustrated in bad marriages. They wish their husbands were more spiritual, more popular, had more leadership qualities, were more authoritative, more patient, better listeners, men of the Word, men of prayer.

And guess what? The pastor fits the bill on every point. The woman may be surprised to find herself falling for him, but once she has, she'll find the fact difficult to hide. And the pastor may at first innocently enjoy being so revered by a woman who needs him. If his wife is nagging him for spending too much time at church, he may begin looking forward to private counseling sessions with a woman who worships him, eats out of his hand, and gives him her full attention.

Pastors and other Christian leaders need hedges as much if not more than the rest of us. If they counsel women at all—and they would, in most cases, do better to assign them to some wise, older women in the church—they should counsel with the door open and the secretary close by. Meetings with any female staff member or parishioner should take place only in public or with at least one other person there.

The dining and traveling hedges should never be trampled when it comes to pastors being with unrelated women. And the only reason their standards are stricter than for us rank-and-file types is that, in most cases, more is at stake.

For all of us, however, the price of suspicion is high, and the price of infidelity is even higher. There are more hedges to plant.

EIGHT

TOUCHY, TOUCHY!

Hedge No. 2—I am careful about touching. While I might shake hands or squeeze an arm or a shoulder in greeting, I embrace only dear friends or relatives, and only in front of others.

I don't know when touching returned to vogue in the United States, but I recall clearly when the encounter group, get-in-touch-with-yourself philosophy finally reached the church. I was in high school in the mid-1960s, and somewhere around that time something new began happening.

Worship became more expressive. People became more emotional. And maybe because there was a significant Jesus People movement heading east from California, and that movement had originated among street people and hippies accustomed to more openness than the rest of society, certain things became more acceptable in the church.

It wasn't all bad. I was visiting a camp when I was about fifteen or sixteen, and after a particularly moving evening of testimonies, singing, and speaking, people were weeping and swaying—as they sang with arms around each others' shoulders. And they finished by giving God an ovation.

That was kind of interesting and different, but what really impressed me was the freedom everyone felt after that to hug each other. I had a girlfriend I didn't mind hugging, but I wasn't crazy about anyone else hugging her. I was shocked to see high school girls hugging camp leaders I knew were married, but it didn't seem to bother anyone else.

That was at a time in my life when I would have enjoyed hugging any female, but still it didn't seem right. When you're that age, you wonder if you can literally control yourself if given the opportunity to embrace a beautiful girl. Suddenly, it seemed okay to hug anybody who was as happy as you were because we were brother and sister in Christ.

I was slow to catch onto the joy of it, and it was hard to keep emotions and feelings in check when you could embrace an adult woman, plus all the girls your own age. It happened all of a sudden, this new freedom, and there was something vaguely spiritual about it.

The rub (pardon the pun) was that—unless I was the only pervert around—I had a good idea that most of the guys my age were less spiritual and more sensual and physical about all this, regardless of their highest ideals. And we all did have high ideals. As I mentioned in chapter two, one of my deepest desires was to remain sexually pure—celibate, virginal—before marriage. This I did, with God's (and a chaste girlfriend's) help, but I confess, this new wrinkle in social behavior was of little assistance.

Say I was a horny teen-ager if you want, but this new openness to embrace was both a dream come true and a nightmare for the two sides of my nature. Christian psychologist James Dobson says that outside of hunger, the most powerful of all the human urges and drives is the sexual appetite. He adds that Christians have the same bio-chemical forces within their bodies that non-Christians do, and I can add from experience that teen-agers, especially males, are bursting with erotic yearnings.

Remember, we're talking about a scant twenty-five years ago. This wasn't the Dark Ages. But how far we've come as a society and as a church since then is staggering. We might not want to admit that maybe things were better before the sexual revolution—even in the church—but we have to ask ourselves: was infidelity, divorce, and scandal as rampant then?

No, I'm not blaming it all on a new openness to touching and hugging, but I know stories of people who fell in love because they enjoyed and looked forward to what began as a spiritual expression of brotherly and sisterly love.

The irony here is that I saw this totally from my own narrow, adolescent viewpoint back then. I told myself that women weren't as interested in sex as men were, and that adults certainly weren't as sexually on fire as teens. I was way too young to know the difference between the sexual responses of males and females.

I knew I could be turned on by the very thought of something sensual. Seeing it was even better. Touching, embracing—well that was just short of making love, wasn't it? What I didn't know then and what statistics, studies, and experts have proven repeatedly since is that women are not turned on sexually in the same way men are. They are less likely to be aroused by thought or even sight. They are aroused more slowly, more subtly, but touch plays a major role.

How could I have known then that embracing a woman who belonged to someone else might be almost the culmination of lust on my part, while it might be the beginning of arousal for her? Am I saying that this new freedom to express ourselves to each other is wrong, sinful, dirty, inappropriate?

No.

I admit that the church needed some thawing, some warming to each other. Men and women particularly needed to loosen up around each other, talk more, get to know each other better, and yes, maybe even touch each other once in awhile.

Remember that back then, except for the healthy exception of certain ethnic groups, men did not touch each other either—except for a formal or macho handshake, back slap, or thump on the rump during a ball game. I can't speak to the effect this new unpretentiousness might have had on men tormented by a bent toward homosexuality, but one such suffering friend of mine admitted it was a terrible temptation.

As I've grown older, I've realized more of the good that has come from the new style. I'm much more comfortable around women, and because it is now appropriate to greet them with a squeeze on the arm or even a warm but proper embrace, I feel better about my relationships. There can be a certain friendly and even spiritual intimacy that doesn't cross the line to impropriety or sensuality. Part of that is due to my own maturity (praise the Lord the testosterone season of youth is pretty much past!), but it is also because of the hedge I'm discussing here.

If I embrace only dear friends or relatives and only in the presence of others, I am not even tempted to make the embrace longer or more impassioned than is appropriate. I like hugging women. It's fun, and it can be friendly. But if I allowed myself to embrace just anyone, even dear friends, in private, I would be less confident of my motives and my subsequent actions.

For instance, what would happen if I just lingered an instant to see what kind of reaction I might get? And let's say that reaction was encouraging. We might both pretend it didn't happen, but what about next time? Would we not be carefully checking each other out to see if what we thought we felt the first time was accurate? And what if it was? At what point would we overtly embrace passionately, silently declaring our feelings for each other?

I don't know, and I don't want to know. That's why I keep such activity public, ensuring its appropriateness.

A Funny Memory

I have a cousin a few years younger than I. She's married and has kids. We've been long-distance buddies for years. Once I was in her state at a writer's conference, and she and her husband invited me for dinner. I waited for her while chatting with a woman from the conference, having idly said my cousin was coming to pick me up.

Oddly, we happened to be discussing this very subject of building hedges around marriages. The woman had read my *Moody Monthly* column on the subject and was telling me some of the hedges she and her husband had planted that fit their careers and lifestyles.

A car slowly pulled up outside, and I thought I recognized my cousin behind the wheel. I said my good-bys, but as I hurried out, my cousin left the car and headed toward me. Youthful, tanned, and in shorts, she was striking and attractive. "Your cousin, huh?" the woman said, laughing. "I'll bet!"

My cousin had a child sleeping in a baby seat in the back, and I was tempted to drag him out and display him to prove we had a chaperone! My cousin was normally a person I would embrace after not having seen her for a long time, but I decided against it for the sake of appearances. She got a good laugh out of the incident.

A Not-So-Funny Memory

Early in my journalism career a young friend of mine went through a trauma. His brother was a wild kind of a guy. The brother lived in Oregon, and though he had had both a drug and alcohol problem in the past, he somehow landed a job as a security guard. One night after work, while at a party, he scuffled with someone, drew his gun, and shot the man, killing him.

My friend, as you can imagine, was distraught. He worried constantly about his brother. Would he be sentenced? Would he commit suicide? Would he get the death penalty? My friend could hardly work, though his job as a copy boy on the midnight shift was important to our paper.

He was a good friend of the managing editor, a man twenty years his senior. The editor and his wife had taken a liking to the young man and encouraged him in his career. Both had been very sympathetic to his worries over his brother and even helped him financially so he could travel to visit him once.

Upon returning from that visit, my friend was convinced that his brother was in worse shape emotionally and psychologically than ever. Rather than help calm his fears, the trip had only upset my friend more. He visited the managing editor's home one night, looking for consolation and advice. The editor was gone. The editor's wife embraced my friend and rocked him as he wept for almost a half hour.

This went on for two more nights in a row before my friend came back with the shocking story that this woman, almost a mother figure to him, had made what he considered a pass at him. We scoffed, assuming he was bragging at best, lying at worst. The next night he said he had "made out" with her for twenty minutes.

She was a woman with a husband who had other priorities. She was a woman who, upon marrying, (as Helen Rowland was quoted in *Reader's Digest* in January of 1955) "exchange[d] the attention of all other men she knew for the inattention of one."* She was starved for passion, and she found it where she could.

My friend was the victim. He was not without fault, but he was weak and vulnerable. Once she had taken advantage of him, there was no turning back. A marriage ended and an affair began. There was no future in it for either of them, but they still played it out.

It all started as an innocent, sympathetic embrace, an act of compassion that turned to passion.

Different Strokes for Different Folks

I realize that this entire subject of hugging and touching may present no problem for some and a very serious prob-

---

* See *The Readers' Digest, Treasury of Modern Quotations* (New York: Readers' Digest Press, 1975), 82.

lem for others. If you have never been turned on by the embrace of a friend, you may think this is ridiculous. For you, perhaps it is. But if a person you embrace or who embraces you has a problem, beware.

There are times, places, and situations where physical touch is the only appropriate response. It's therapeutic, loving, and kind. There are other instances where the same response is overkill.

A dear friend of ours recently suffered a terrible tragedy, losing the two people closest to her in the world to an accident in which she also was severely injured. This friend is close enough that I feel free to embrace her in public regularly. Now that she was in the deepest physical and emotional agony a person could endure, I didn't think twice about holding her hand as we talked or even resting my hand on her head as I would with a child in pain. My wife was also there, and this seemed the most logical and normal behavior.

In another context, at another time, a different set of actions would be appropriate. I love this woman in the purest non-romantic sense. I felt deeply for her and wanted her to know it. In another situation or circumstance I would want to guard appearances by responding differently.

The matter of touching and being touched, embracing and being embraced, is as much a matter of common sense and decency as it is of ethnic background and custom. Because of the way I was raised, I tread carefully in this area. If it doesn't happen to be an issue with you, I recommend only that you be sensitive to the attitudes and interpretations of those you choose to touch.

NINE

SOME COMPLIMENTS DON'T PAY

Hedge No. 3—If I pay a compliment, it is on clothes or hairstyle, not on the person herself. Commenting on a pretty outfit is much different, in my opinion, than telling a woman that she herself looks pretty.

Am I dealing here only with semantics? I think not. I still remember the first time, in the eighth grade, I mustered the courage to tell a girl "You look sharp today." I was so nervous, and gushing that compliment was so disabling, that I never thought to study her reaction.

She thanked me, but clearly I had made her feel uncomfortable, too. Was she as affected as I was? I mean, I was a person so afraid of girls at that point that even adding "How are ya?" at the end of a greeting was too much to consider.

Girls might call me by name and say hi. I would say, "Hi." They would add, "How are ya?" I'd say "Fine," and keep moving. Why didn't I add, "How are you?"

Conversation, my mother always told me, was like a tennis match. "Someone lobs one to you; you lob it back."

But I was in high school before I marshaled the courage to do that. The results were amazing. A girl I thought was gorgeous greeted me and asked how I was. I said fine and asked her how she was. She assured me she was great and that she was glad I was fine. And she smiled at me. That alone was enough of a payoff. I had a limited enough self-image to know there was no future in a relationship with her. After all, I hardly knew her, but having a normal, polite, albeit empty conversation with her provided its own euphoric rush.

So you can see what an accomplishment it had been in junior high to have summoned the fortitude to actually tell a girl she looked sharp. I lived on that high for days, realizing only after a week or so that the girl was carefully avoiding me. Had I upset her? Scared her? Made her think I was interested in her? Nothing was worse at that age than having someone after you in whom you were not interested. I wasn't cool or "in," wasn't a sharp dresser, and didn't have money. I was invisible. The only girls I attracted were those who knew they couldn't land someone impressive. When they chased me, I ran. And now I knew how they felt. I even sent that girl a valentine card, one my brother had dreamed up. It included several small slips of paper with various flowers drawn on them. The card itself was a poem, instructing the recipient to send back to me one of the flowers as a message. For instance, "If I am the one you chose, send me back the big, red rose." There were flowers that would tell me to be patient, to wait, to keep trying, and there was even a dandelion with the verse, "If I waste my time in tryin', send me back the dandelion."

I waited and waited for some response. I was being ignored and even avoided at school, and it got to the point where I would have been happy even to get the dandelion back. I merely wanted to know if she was aware of my existence. Maybe she had never received the card. The worst possible reaction was no reaction, and that's what I got. Valerie, if you're out there, I need to tell you I'm happily married, and it's too late. If the rose merely got lost in the mail and you thought *I* had ignored *you* after that, what can I say except I'm sorry. (I wish I could remember her last name. She sure looked sharp that day.)

Lessons

In retrospect, I realize what I did wrong there. Had Valerie been pining away for me, perhaps my compliment on how sharp she looked would have thrilled her. But since my approach was clearly a surprise, I should have emphasized the clothes and not the person. I should have been just slightly less personal, which is what I need to do now. I don't have the right to tell a woman how *she* looks, though it might be nice and appropriate to comment on her clothes or hair.

I base part of this hedge on my own reaction to how men talk to my wife. Dianna is tall, dark, and stunning—a head turner. It makes me proud to see men do a double take when they see her. If they keep staring, though, I stare right back until they notice that she's with me.

Dianna is one of those typical beautiful women who is unaware of her beauty and its impact. If I thought she was looking for compliments it might bother me, but I'm used to the fact that she gets many. And I know she is truly beautiful as opposed to merely sexy, because she gets just as many compliments from women as from men. (In my experience women compliment each other only on their beauty, not on their seductivity.)

For some reason, it does not bother me if a man comments on my wife's hair or makeup or clothes. But if he should say that *she* looks pretty or is gorgeous or beautiful, that is too personal. Interestingly, either kind of compliment makes her uncomfortable, but she agrees that the personal approach is worse.

As a hedge, I stop short of the purely personal compliment, because you can never be sure of the reaction. Some women would be offended at such familiarity, and men who talk to women that way tend to get reputations for it. I know a man who is known not only for talking to and about women that way, but also for hanging around them whenever he gets the chance. He always chats with the best-looking woman at work, church, or at a party. At conventions, he spends most of his time at the swimming pool talking to the best-looking women. I don't know him well enough to know whether his marriage is strong, but you can imagine what people will think if a rumor of infidelity ever begins making the rounds. Innocent or not, he won't have a chance to survive it.

I don't get complimented about my looks, but occasionally I'll wear something that people like, and they say so. If a woman tells me she likes my tie, jacket, hat, or even my beard, I don't wonder if she's on the prowl or frustrated by a bad marriage. I merely feel complimented about my taste.

Hearing Voices

On the rare occasion when a woman compliments me on the way *I* look, I confess I'm uncomfortable. Like anyone else, I have certain needs in my life, and among those are what Dr. James Dobson calls emotional requirements: love, acceptance, belonging, caring, and tenderness. My goal is to seek the fulfillment of those needs within the context of my own marriage.

Dr. Dobson says there are certain voices that would lure a person away from the straight life—the life of giving yourself to your spouse and children, working, paying the bills—toward infidelity. These are pleasure ("Come on, have fun, life is passing you by!"), romanticism (someone who cares, someone interested in you as a person, someone who wants to love you), sex (the pure pleasure of the physical act), and ego needs (someone finds you attractive for your mind, tastes, or talents).

Dr. Dobson ranks sex at the low end of the scale of these reasons and puts ego needs at the top, for both men and women. For women, he says, romanticism may be a close second, depending on the health of the marriage, and sex may be more important to men than to women because of the differences in biological makeup. The late James L. Johnson, on the flyleaf of his book *What Every Woman Should Know About a Man**, called sex "the strange and mysterious drive of the God-given chemistry

---

* Grand Rapids: The Zondervan Corporation, 1977

that had shaped nations, destroyed kingdoms, and brought ruin or ecstasy to millions from the beginning of time."

The problem with these voices that would lure us away from the straight life is that they are lying voices. They promise something other than simply another straight life, but that is not possible. If we run off with another spouse—even if we do find more pleasure, more romance, more sex, and more of our ego needs fulfilled—there is still a straight life that has to be dealt with. In fact, it may be more burdensome than the one we left because of the alimony and child-care expenses from the previous marriage. As Dr. Dobson says, "The grass may be greener on the other side of the fence, but it still has to be mowed."

Go Ahead, Make Her Day

The problem with ego needs and the need for romance, especially in a woman's life, is that they are hidden, unseen factors that men need to take into consideration when talking to women. We may innocently think it'll make a woman's day if we pay her a compliment that borders on the personal. So, rather than telling her that her sweater is beautiful and asking if she made it (implying that if she made it she's incredible and if she bought it she has great taste), we tell her *she* looks great in it.

How do we know that perhaps the pleasure and romance and even the sex and ego strokes haven't long since evaporated from her marriage? How do we know that she hasn't been longing for just this sort of attention from her husband? How do we know she hasn't given up on ever getting any more strokes from him, and that this very personal approach from us may reach deep needs of which she is hardly aware?

I want to be careful not to make women in bad marriages sound so weak and dependent that they live and die for any personal interest on the part of other men. But in individual cases, we don't know, do we? It never ceases to amaze me when I hear about the latest wife-abuse victim or wife who has been cheated on.

Several years ago a visiting preacher friend counseled the middle-aged wife of a pillar in our church. Her husband, a leading evangelical, had been in the ministry more than forty years.

The story she told the evangelist was incredible. She had been a psychological prisoner in her own home for decades and had been physically abused every few weeks during her entire marriage. She was nearly suicidal, but she had heard something in the evangelist's sermon that gave her a glimmer of hope. My friend told her there was nothing he could do for her until she was prepared to tell someone in authority—her pastor, her husband's superiors, or the police—about her husband. She was unwilling to do that.

Her husband is dead now, and I have lost track of her. Sadly, however, her daughter must have suffered all those years, too. A few years after seemingly marrying happily and starting a family—and several years before her father died—she disappeared for a few days and committed suicide a hundred miles from home.

I share that sordid story to make the point that we never know what kinds of wounds and pains a person carries to church every Sunday. The woman in the account above would probably not have been vulnerable to an approach by any man except for an extremely kind, gentle, godly person. But what about the others? What about those we know just as little about?

No doubt a case could be made for the fact that some women wouldn't know the difference between a compliment of their hair or dress and of themselves as persons. However, there *is* a difference, even if it registers only subliminally. Planting a hedge that allows you to compliment only a woman's taste in styles and clothes frees you to be friendly, outgoing, and encouraging to women without being suspected of anything worse.

Best Friends

Years ago I had a boss who told me a story that illustrates the dangers I've been discussing in this chapter. A friend of his was suspected of taking too much interest in a female teacher at the school where he coached. Bill insisted there was nothing going on, but as rumor after rumor persisted, my friend felt obligated to confront him.

"If there's nothing going on between you and Nancy," my friend said, "why don't you quit spending so much time with her?"

"I like her," Bill said. "And she likes me. Is there anything wrong with having a friend of the opposite sex?"

"It depends on how your wife feels about it," my boss said.

"She hates it, but she's never been a friend to me."

My boss counseled him to break off the relationship. Within six months Bill and Nancy had divorced their spouses and married each other. Bill finally confessed to my boss that they had been intimate almost from the beginning of their relationship. "It all started with my telling her how pretty she looked every day," he said. "She said she had been starved for that kind of attention, because she worked so hard at looking good and no one, she emphasized *no one,* ever seemed to notice."

"Except you," my boss said.

"Except me," Bill said smiling. He was thrilled. He had found the girl of his dreams. No matter that two marriages and five children had been caught in the whirlwind. And neither Bill nor Nancy pledged that they would be truer to each other than to their first spouses. Bill never said he would quit complimenting women personally, and Nancy never said she would quit looking for the same from men other than her husband. For Bill to have kept the second marriage intact, he would have had to realize he was competing with anyone who thought his wife looked good and had the guts to tell her.

Apparently, he couldn't keep up with the competition. The marriage lasted fewer than four years, and it was she who left him for an older man. (How long would you give that relationship?)

There was something about being dumped that brought Bill to his senses. He realized what he had done to his wife, and he seemed remorseful. He pleaded with his first wife to take him back. Even though she felt that, as a divorced woman, she was not free to marry anyone else, she didn't trust him. She was still in such pain over what he did to her that she asked for time to think it over before taking him back.

He couldn't wait, and he married again. Chaos.

There Is a Way

Sometimes it feels great to compliment a woman other than your wife in a personal way, and you sense it would be a good thing to do. In cases like that I talk it over with Dianna first. We had a friend who was dumped by her husband, and he tried to justify taking up with another married woman by telling anyone who would listen that, despite her image, his wife was a shrew—cold, mean, unattractive, and dull.

Maybe behind closed doors she was all that, but my wife and I felt we knew her well enough and had seen her in enough situations to know that she was sweet, spiritual, a good mother, and a loyal and loving wife. She may not have been the hottest thing in town or the most fashionable dresser, but she had certainly done nothing that would justify her husband's adultery.

After planning and almost scripting our approach, Dianna and I made sure we ran into her after church one Sunday night. With my arm around my own wife but looking directly into that suffering woman's eyes, I said, "You're not going to let what Benny says convince you that you're not pretty or attractive or exciting, are you?"

She blushed and shook her head. I would not have felt free to say that to her without my wife at my side, nodding her assent. And Dianna added, "We know how much you have to offer, and if Benny can't see that, he's just wrong. If he follows through with this, it'll be his loss, not yours."

As a rule we make it a point not to take sides in separations and divorces, but when there is flagrant adultery, we feel little loyalty to the offending party, friend or not.

To quote James Dobson once more, "Marriage is an institution designed to meet individual needs."* The key

---

* "The Lure of Infidelity," Audio cassette from Focus on the Family, (1978).

is for husband and wife to meet each other's needs and for other people to mind their own business. Let me meet my own wife's need for pleasure, romance, sex, and ego strokes, and I'll let you meet your wife's.

TEN

LOOKING DOWN THE BARREL OF A LOADED GUN

Hedge No. 4—I avoid flirtation or suggestive conversation, even in jest.

My dad, a police chief, firearms expert, and marksman, once told me that prayer is like looking down the barrel of a loaded gun. "You're likely to get what you're asking for."

I put flirtation and suggestive conversation in the same category as a loaded gun. Maybe that's because I believe in the power of words, written and spoken. Have you ever noticed that compliments and flattery are always heard? People have reminded me of compliments I have given years before and almost forgotten. They remember criticism too, but flattery all the more.

Idle flirting gets people in trouble because the other person needs and wants attention so badly. Not many years ago I slipped from behind this hedge, not intending to flirt but rather to be funny. It didn't get me in serious trouble, but I was certainly reminded of the reason for my hedge.

On a business trip a woman colleague and I were going to go out to dinner with a male associate of ours. When she came to pick me up, she was dressed and made up in flashy, coordinated colors that demanded some comment. I should have just said something about her clothes, but instead—since she is always a good audience for my humor—I said the first funny thing that popped into my mind: "My, don't you look delicious."

She laughed, and I hoped she knew I meant that her colors reminded me of fruit, and not that I wished to devour her. As soon as our third party arrived, she told him what I had said. He gave me a look that would have put a wart on a gravestone, but what could I say? I couldn't deny it, and it was too late to explain.

Men, of course, are just as susceptible to flattery as women. Most people think that the man in Proverbs heading down the road of destruction to the harlot's bed had followed his lust for sex. Surely that was part of it, but the text indicates that he also was seduced by her words. Proverbs 7:4, 5 says, "Say to wisdom, 'You are my sister,' and call understanding your nearest kin, that they may keep you from the immoral woman, from the seductress *who flatters with her words*" [emphasis mine].

And Proverbs 7:10 and 21 says:

> And there a woman met him, with the attire of a harlot, and a crafty heart.
>
> With her *enticing speech* she caused him to yield, with her *flattering lips* she seduced him [emphasis mine].

Keep Humor in Its Place

Everyone knows that funny people speak the truth through humor. They may exaggerate how upset they are that someone is late by looking at their watch and saying, "Oh, glad you could make it!" But beneath the joke is a barb of truth. The jokester has slipped in a little lecture without having had to embarrass anyone by saying, "Hey, pal, we agreed on six o'clock and now here you come at six-thirty! What's the deal? Get your act together!"

But the same thing happens when someone tries to be funny in a flirting manner. A man tells a woman, "Why don't we run off together? Tell that good-for-nothing husband of yours you got a better offer, huh?"

How's a woman supposed to react to that? The first time she may think it's funny because it's so far out of the realm of possibility. Each succeeding time Mr. Comedian says something like that, it gets a little more irritating. That is, unless the woman has always been attracted to him and has problems at home. Then she might hope there's some truth behind the humor.

Often, there is. The only time a funny flirter is totally putting someone on is when he throws his arm around a particularly old or homely woman and tries to give her a thrill by saying something she's probably never heard before. "Gorgeous! Where have you been all my life?"

Women like that know better than to believe such drivel, but they may long to hear it anyway. A colleague of mine once toyed with just such a woman by caressing her cheek with his hand. "I'm melting," she said, and I sensed that she meant it.

The real danger comes when the man is pretending to be teasing, but he'd really love to flirt in just the way he's exaggerating. A woman may not suspect the truth behind his humor, and if she responds in kind, there is the opportunity for misunderstanding. Or worse, she may indeed suspect that he means it, and then there is the opportunity for real understanding.

Such a tragedy occurred at a church in Michigan where a couple flirted humorously for almost ten years. They did this in front of everybody, including their spouses, who laughed right along with them. The flirters were never seen alone together, because they never *were* alone together.

Then came the day when the woman's husband was sick and in the hospital. She needed rides back and forth, and her friend and his wife provided them. No one suspected anything, but on one of those rare occasions when it was just the man doing the driving, the wife of the sick man told him how difficult and cold her husband had been for years.

The flirters began to see each other on the sly until the day came when she told him she had always hoped he'd meant what he said when he had teased her about how wonderful she was, how good she looked, and how he wished he'd met her before she was married. Whether he really meant it was irrelevant now that she had declared herself. The fact was, he admitted later, that this was what he had unquestionably wanted all along. He would never have made the first move, however. He had hidden his true desires behind a cloak of humor. A little crisis, a little honesty, and suddenly years of innocent flirting had blossomed into an affair.

Innocent Humor

I worked at a camp one summer during my high school years. One week one of the women counselors, about a year older than I, shared my last name. We were not related and had never seen each other before. When we were introduced, we had not even made much of an issue over the name duplication. While Jenkins is not as common as Smith or Jones, neither is it as unique as Higginbottham or Szczepanik.

One night after the campers were in bed a bunch of us staffers and a few of the counselors, Miss Jenkins included, were watching a football game on television. A couple of the guys started kidding Miss Jenkins and me about being married. We were both so young and naive and insecure that we just blushed and hoped the running gag would run out of gas.

For some reason I had to leave the impromptu party before the game was over, and as I headed for the door, someone said, "Hey, Jenkins, aren't you takin' yer wife with ya?"

I got this urge to show the crowd that I could be just as funny as they and that I was a good sport, so I turned and pointed at her. "No, but I want you home in bed in fifteen minutes."

I was out the door and ten feet from the TV cabin when I heard the hooting and hollering. I had not intended even to imply anything risqué. I had merely been trying to go along with the joke, and instead of speaking to the girl the way a husband would to a wife, I had spoken to her as father to daughter. Of course, everyone took my wanting her home in bed the wrong way, and with my reputation for enjoying a funny line, I knew I would never live it down. In fact, if I tried to go back and explain, no one would even believe me. They would wonder why I didn't want to take the credit for such a great joke.

The girl was as sweet and chaste as most counselors would be at a camp like that, and the last thing I wanted her to think was that I had been inappropriate and had gotten a cheap laugh at her expense. A hundred feet from the cabin, still hearing the laughter, I knew I had to go back.

When I opened the door, no one even noticed me. Something had happened on the game that had everyone's attention. I was glad to see that Miss Jenkins wasn't sitting there weeping with her head in her hands. When I called her name and she looked up, so did everyone else, and the snickering began again. I wished they had been laughing at me for saying such a stupid thing, but I knew they were laughing because I had gotten away with such a saucy line.

"Could I see you for a minute?" I asked, and the room fell deathly silent.

I'll never forget her response as long as I live. "I'm not too sure," she said. It was the funniest comeback I could imagine in that situation, and I wish I'd anticipated it. If my original line had been intentional, I would still have always thought hers was better, especially on the spur of the moment.

The place erupted again, and I winced self-consciously, knowing that I appeared to deserve that. I was grateful when she bounced to her feet and followed me out into the darkness. I had the impression she knew what I was going to say.

"You need to know that I didn't mean that the way it sounded," I said.

"I know," she said.

"You do?"

"Uh-huh."

"I don't think anyone else understands that."

"Maybe not, but I do. I've seen you around, heard you be funny. That's not your style. At first I was embarrassed and disappointed, but I caught a glimpse of your face as you hurried out, and I knew."

"Your comeback in there was priceless," I said.

"I couldn't pass it up. But I knew you were back to apologize, so I figured I could say something and apologize for it at the same time."

"I'm sorry," I said. "I didn't mean to embarrass you."

"Accepted," she said. "I know. And I'm sorry too, though I admit I *did* mean to embarrass you."

I laughed and she added, "We Jenkins have to stick together, you know."

Strangely, we didn't see any more of each other after that than we would have otherwise. She was older and was not on staff, so she had her crowd and I had mine. I had learned a lesson, though. I knew to be more careful about teasing in a flirting manner. I also learned how wonderful and forgiving and insightful some women can be. Funny, too.

By the Same Token

Along these same lines, I have made it a practice—and can probably list this among my hedges—of not making my wife the butt of jokes. There are enough things to make fun of and enough funny topics without going for easy laughs at the expense of your spouse.

One of the reasons for this, besides my memory of how bad I felt about unintentionally ribbing my teen-age camp "wife," is that I would never want Dianna to think I was trying to tell her something serious under the guise of humor. We have made it a policy to speak honestly and forthrightly with each other about anything that bothers us.

We give the lie to that pontification that married couples who never fight are probably as miserable and phony as those who fight all the time. We love each other. We don't always agree, and we get on each other's nerves occasionally, but neither of us likes tension in the air. We compete to see who can apologize first and get things talked out. We follow the biblical injunction to never let the sun go down upon our wrath (Ephesians 4:26).

When a group of adult Christians decides it would be healthy to be honest and to share some of their most embarrassing or petty fights, we always confess that we'll either have to pass or make one up. Slammed doors, cold shoulders, silent treatments, and walking out just are not part of our routine. I think this comes as a result of being careful with our tongues.

Just as I don't want to make the mistake of flirting in jest or being suggestive in conversation with anyone but my wife, I want to watch what I say to her, too. Scripture has a lot to say about the power of the tongue and the spoken word. Proverbs 18:21 says that death and life "are in the power of the tongue," and Proverbs 21:23 says, "Whoever guards his mouth and tongue keeps his soul from troubles."

Proverbs 28:23 says that, "He who rebukes a man will find more favor afterward than he who flatters with the tongue." In the New Testament, James says that the tongue is a little member, but that it boasts great things. "See how great a forest a little fire kindles!" (James 3:5)

Flattery, flirtation, suggestive jesting, and what we say to our own spouses are all shades of the same color. Beware the power of the tongue.

E L E V E N

MEMORIES

Hedge No. 5—I remind my wife often—in writing and orally—that I remember my wedding vows: "Keeping you only unto me for as long as we both shall live . . . " Dianna is not the jealous type, nor has she ever demanded such assurances from me. She does, however, appreciate my rules and my observance of them.

People seem to make their wedding vows so cavalierly nowadays that you have to wonder if they have any idea what they're saying. Census figures show that one of every four marriages performed in 1931–33 ended in divorce. By the mid-'50s the rate had jumped to one in three. By 1971 it had hit 41 percent.* Everybody knows that the figure passed the 50 percent mark early in the 1980s.

It may be naive to think that people would remain true to their vows just by repeating them frequently, but

---

* *The Readers' Digest, Treasury of Modern Quotations* (New York: Readers' Digest Press, 1975), 83.

who knows? At least couples might come to understand what they said in a ceremony before God, friends, and spouse.

Practical Suggestions

There are many creative ways to remind your spouse and yourself of your wedding vows, and they can be adapted to any budget. Try surprising your wife with a progressive search that culminates in a trip somewhere special. If you can afford it, take her out of the country. If you can't, drive to the next town for a weekend at a hotel. Or even just to McDonalds.

Set it up this way:

Write out slips that contain your wedding vows, particularly those that refer to remaining sexually faithful, in a rhyme or even a little story format. At the end of each slip, leave a clue for where your wife can find the next one. Then hide them around the house and in the garage.

Mail the first one home. It might say, "Keeping you—" and then "Look for another message in the freezer."

When she looks in the freezer she finds another slip that reads, "—only unto me—" and "Look for another message in the car."

In the car is a slip that reads, "—for as long—" and points her to the mantle over the fireplace. There she finds a note that says, "—as we both—" and "Look for another message in the junk drawer." There is a message that reads, "—shall live." There you might also plant her plane ticket or hotel reservation or baby sitting certificate or McDonalds gift certificate.

It can be just as effective, though maybe not as much fun, simply to call her at home or at work, and tell her, "I made this vow ______ years/months/days ago, and I still mean it: 'I will keep you only unto myself for as long as we both shall live, or until Christ, who has saved us by His grace, returns to take us unto Himself forever.'"

Sending your vows in a telegram or mailgram can be effective. You might even have someone do it in calligraphy or have it printed so you can decoupage it. I've heard of people having their vows written in icing on a cake, chiseled into a rock, burned into wood, even written in moist dirt in the front yard. A friend of mine spent a couple of hours forming the letters to his vows in tiny bits of twig, then set them up on the cement slab in front of the door of his house, only to see his wife miss their significance and sweep them off the porch onto the grass.

Sometimes I like to just tell Dianna that I remember my vows and that she is the only woman I have ever slept with, and the only one I ever wish to sleep with. I usually add my own sentiments on anniversary, valentine, and birthday cards, too. I don't think she ever tires of hearing me reiterate my vows. I know I never get tired of hearing or saying them.

What's Good for the Goose

The sad fact is that there is simply not enough emphasis on wedding vows any more. We need to face it: this is one of the most significant problems in modern marriage. I've never understood the long-standing double standard that seems to wink at males' infidelity while holding women in contempt for the same offense. Of course, the breaking of a sacred vow should not be tolerated for either sex, but there is a boys-will-be-boys mentality that allows some men—even Christians—to have occasional or long-standing mistresses their entire married lives.

As we've seen countless marriages break up during our nearly twenty years together, Dianna and I have talked seriously about this issue. Divorce is not in our vocabulary, but we have discussed whether either of us could forgive the other for the ultimate in unfaithfulness and betrayal.

Early in our marriage Dianna told me she didn't think she was capable of forgiving sexual unfaithfulness. Though I had, of course, never considered violating my vows, it was impressive to hear that. I tried to imagine the shoe on the other foot and decided the same. The thought of sleeping with my wife after she had been unfaithful was inconceivable. It still is, but both of our views have grown on this subject.

We have seen friends' and relatives' marriages shattered by adultery, and yet we have also counseled wives to forgive husbands and take them back. Regaining trust after adultery still seems impossible, and neither of us has come to the point where we will say unequivocally that we could take back the other after unfaithfulness. We admit, though, that there are other things to consider.

For instance, we have seen that adultery is usually not the major problem in bad marriages. It is a result of a bad marriage or a symptom of a bad marriage. It may be the worst thing that can happen to a marriage, but it is rarely *the* basic problem. We hope and trust and believe and pray that any of our discussions about this subject are academic in our own marriage because we work so hard at it, but adultery does occasionally invade even seemingly solid marriages.

Take the case of Gordon MacDonald, the former pastor and Christian leader who stepped down from the presidency of Inter-Varsity Christian Fellowship a few years ago after his adultery was revealed. His wife and some trusted advisers already knew of his sin and also of his repentance. When it came to light, however, he realized that resigning was the only way to protect the reputation of Inter-Varsity and keep them from extended controversy.

Anyone who knew MacDonald knew he had been a model husband and father. Even his wife and children said so. Thus the shocking moral lapse was clearly not the result of a pattern in his life or of a bad marriage. He admits that during a period of burnout and extreme fatigue he allowed a friendship to become immoral, and though the illicit relationship was no more than a one-night stand, he apparently sincerely repented.

Gail MacDonald not only forgave Gordon but has also said she would not dwell on his short period of unfaithfulness. To their credit, neither discounted that he had sinned, that his actions were unacceptable, or that he needed to repent and ask forgiveness of God and all parties affected. There are those who feel he has forever disqualified himself from the ministry (he was subsequently re-commissioned by one of his former churches), but what I want to deal with here is the forgiveness aspect.

If Gordon was truly repentant, did Gail have a choice as a Christian to do anything but forgive him and welcome him back? While many believe that adultery is Biblical grounds for divorce, surely divorce is not mandated when the offending party is remorseful and wants to reconcile.

Therefore, even though both Dianna and I cannot imagine finding within ourselves the wherewithal to forgive the other should adultery ever disgrace and defile our marriage, clearly the Biblical, Christian response to a repentant sinner is forgiveness. In ourselves, in our flesh, this would probably not be possible. Only through Christ can divine, unconditional love find forgiveness for a spouse who has foisted the filthiest pollution on a marriage.

Even as Dianna and I continue to struggle with the proper response—and, as I say, continue also to pray against such a problem and work toward a marriage that will not allow it—we counsel those who have been victimized to forgive the offending spouse if he or she is willing to reconcile. We can only pray that we could be as charitable to each other, as inconceivable as that is to us now.

One thing is certain. Marriages in which the ultimate loss of trust has been suffered can never be the same. We can only imagine what a wife who has taken back a husband who slept with another woman, or vice versa, must go through when that offending spouse wants to enjoy the marriage bed again. How long would it be—if ever—before either could forget that the vows had been broken, that one of them had not kept the other only unto himself or herself? Could deep, abiding trust ever be fully regained? No wonder few marriages survive such an onslaught.

Although I would probably want more than anything to reconcile with my wife after such a failure, I certainly wouldn't be able to blame her if she simply was not able to forgive that outrage, that transgression of her trust. And while if I was the offended party I cannot fathom being able to put her sin out of my mind, I'd like to think I would not turn away my truly repentant wife whom I love.

Even considering that jumble of horrifying emotions is so distasteful that all it does is make me want to emphasize again the whole reason for this book. Again I need to say that adultery is usually a result or symptom of a marriage with weaknesses throughout. If it takes occasionally just running through your mind's eye being caught or having to confess to your wife that you have been unfaithful, then I recommend that exercise.

You won't find it pleasant. Imagine breaking down as you tell her, hoping she'll understand, seeing her turn cold and hurt and dark, not wanting to be touched or to hear anymore. My guess is that the typical woman won't want to see her husband's tears of grief and remorse right away. He will tumble off whatever pedestal he may have been on, and should she ever find it within herself, by the grace of God, to forgive him and take him back, it will not be without deep pain and suffering.

Imagine, just imagine, what that would do to your wife. Plant hedges wide and deep and tall against any weakness you may have. Remind yourself what price you would have to pay for a brief season of carnal fun. Study what is wrong with you or your relationship with your wife that would allow you even to consider such a drastic breach of her trust.

Dianna and I had college friends who were married ten years and had two sons when we first got wind that there was trouble. The wife suspected her husband was seeing another woman. We stood by her, helped her find out, confronted him, heard the denials, and then learned the awful truth: It was true.

He was unrepentant, hostile, and flagrant. He had complaints about his wife, but none justified this complete setting aside of his morals and values. She kept fighting for him, wanting him back. We warned her that until he gave up the other woman and—in essence—came back on his knees, she should be slow to open her arms. Maybe we were intruding rather than helping at that point, but she received similar counsel from others.

Still, she was desperate. She couldn't stand the thought of losing him to someone else. No, she was not the woman he had married. She had given birth to both sons within a year of each other, and she had grown weary and harried trying to keep up with them. Maybe she had become shrill, and maybe she had neglected him a bit, but he had never grown up either. Now he played most of the time and was gone more than he was home. And now this. Another woman.

She moved in with her aunt and took the boys with her. He begged her to come back, promising to change his ways. It was all she wanted to hear. She set conditions: Give up the other woman, spend time at home, don't expect Olympic sex after this rupture of my trust, and grow up.

The first night they spent together, he got a call from the other woman. "Take that call and I'm out of here," his wife told him.

"Just some loose ends," he assured her, and he talked on the phone for a half hour. Then he left. "Just getting some stuff, settling accounts. Don't worry. It's over."

He was gone all night and still tried to tell her nothing had happened. But he had pushed his wife past the brink. She packed up the boys and all her belongings and moved out. Even while he was again trying to plead with her to take him back, a friend saw his car in front of his girlfriend's house all night. The friend left a note, berating him for living a lie. That finally brought him to his senses.

From what we could tell, he had finally truly repented. He'd come back to God, cut off the relationship, and done everything he could to win back his wife.

But do you know what? It was too late. If she had been Jesus she might have forgiven him seventy times seven, and there were those who felt she was being cold and unforgiving and even unchristian. Sadly, he had pushed her too far. I'm not saying she was right, but she got to the place of rage, and suddenly she could believe nothing he said and could trust nothing he promised. She could only suspect everything he did.

That story is ten years old now and both partners have been married again. She has divorced for the second time. We're talking about Christian people here. Adultery creates chaos. Adulterers lie. Victims get angry. There are human limits to forgiveness, even among Christians.

Somehow, some way, we who have remained true to our spouses need to do something to ensure that we remain that way. That means working on our weaknesses, shoring up our strengths, pouring our lives into each other, and planting hedges. We must avoid the mess of adultery and divorce and the besmirching of the reputation of Christ. The time is long past for us to worry about people snickering at us for being prudish or Victorian or puritanical.

Treat this blight on marriage as the epidemic that it is. Flee. Plant a hedge. Do something. Anything. Don't become a sad statistic.

T W E L V E

QUALITY TIME VS. QUANTITY TIME

Hedge No. 6—From the time I get home from work until the children go to bed, I do no writing or office work. This gives me lots of time with the family and for my wife and me to continue to court and date.

Something subtle but unusual happened to me after Dianna and I had been married for about a year. I had recently left the field of secular journalism and begun working for Scripture Press. Among my duties was the responsibility to interview people for stories for the Sunday school papers.

Coincidentally, several of my interviews during a short span were with middle-aged men. Their stories were all different, but eventually we got around to the subjects of home and marriage and family. Five or six of these men shared with me their regrets about those areas of their lives. Their marriages had been fine and their children had turned out okay, but every one of them regretted not having spent more time at home. They had a lot of "if onlys."

"If only I'd realized that my daughter's recital was more important than the big real estate deal . . . "

"If only I could have proved to my son how proud I was of his athletic ability by showing up at his games . . ."

"If only my wife had known before she died how much I enjoyed talking with her and traveling with her . . . "

Someone has said that no one has ever been heard to say on his deathbed, "I wish I'd spent more time at the office."

These discussions of regret over misplaced priorities during the sunny years of their careers—which always seem to coincide with the growing up years of a man's family—had little to do with their stories and didn't wind up in the pages of Scripture Press' Sunday school papers. But I sensed God had put me in contact with these men for a reason: they were all sending me the same message. I was barely twenty-two years old, but I caught the drift.

I remember lengthy discussions with Dianna about it. We wouldn't have our first child until we'd been married four-and-a-half years, and that gave us lots of time to set goals, policies, and priorities. We wanted to be good parents and avoid regrets.

We decided that once the children came along, regardless of their ages, I would do no writing and no office business between the time I got home from work and the time the kids went to bed. (I've been accused of putting them to bed at four-thirty!)

In the beginning the biggest benefit was to Dianna, who had someone to take over feeding and changing and entertaining a baby while she finally had time to fix dinner. Sometimes baby Dallas was sleeping when I got home, but that didn't count; he had to be down for the night before I felt free to get into my own projects.

As Dallas got older and Chad came along (two-and-a-half years later), he learned to take for granted that I would be around during that time of the day. I didn't insist that the boys take advantage of me or even play with me. I just wanted them to get used to the fact that I was theirs to talk to, to play with, or even to ignore.

During that period I learned that the idea of *Quality Time* was an evil lie. Some experts pushed the idea that successful overachievers, those we call Yuppies today, could have children and be guilt-free about the little time they were able to devote to them. The remedy was Quality Time. Sort of like one-minute parenting. It went like this: Be sure to make what little time you are able to spend with your child Quality Time.

What garbage. I've seen the results of kids who were given only Quality Time. The problem is that kids don't know the difference. What they need is time—all they can get. Quantity time *is* quality time, whether you're discussing the meaning of the cosmos or just climbing on dad.

There are times I wish my kids knew how wonderful I was being about all this. I don't know too many fathers who give their kids at least two-and-a-half hours a day, and there certainly aren't any other fathers who play ball with the whole neighborhood every summer afternoon.

I confess that this is not all just for the kids' benefit. I can't imagine missing out on some of the growth experiences, the funny and touching things they say, and even being there in times of crisis when I could easily be somewhere else.

There came a point in our lives when Dallas, at about age four, told me he wished he had a new dad. Like who? I asked him. Like the man down the street, he told me. I knew exactly who he was talking about and why.

The man down the street came home so infrequently that he got a royal welcome every time he did. And he was usually feeling so guilty about his drinking or topless-bar hopping or compulsive spending that he brought gifts for everyone. What a guy! What a dad! He must be super to get that kind of reception and be so generous!

I couldn't explain the distinctions to Dallas until he was old enough to understand why the man down the street left his wife a note for breakfast one morning, telling her she would find him in the garage with the car running. He had committed suicide.

So What?

What does all this have to do with marital hedges?

Hedges can do wonders for a family, and this policy of spending mega-blocks of time with the kids each day has turned into rich benefits for Dianna and me, too. Our time together is more relaxed, less hurried, less pressured, less obligatory. We have learned to just be with each other, to be used to having each other around. We don't have to talk, plan, schedule, or make appointments with each other. We know each other's schedules, and we count on when the other will be available. Dianna adds that she enjoys a tremendous sense of satisfaction and well-being when I am devoting time to the kids. She has never felt left out or jealous of the time, especially since she and I also spend a lot of time together.

At the time of this writing our boys are fourteen, almost twelve, and seven. They are old enough to figure out that their relationship with their parents is out of the ordinary, at least as it relates to the amount of time spent. We hardly ever miss one of their school or sports-related events, and we will not be gone from home more than a certain number of days without taking them with us. Our trip to Africa this past summer was one of the richest family times we've ever had.

More importantly, the kids can see a difference in our marriage, too. They know we're still affectionate and in love and demonstrative about it even after all these years. The older two boys especially are at ages where they want to know the whys and wherefores of all our ideas and behavior, so I've been able to tell them about our hedges and why we feel they're so important.

They're intrigued by it all, even though it probably won't make total sense to them until they are in love or married. But having my sons know of my hedges serves almost as another hedge. Just like my friend who carries pictures of his wife and daughters as a hedge on business trips, I carry the knowledge that my kids are aware of my concern for our marriage. They would be front-line victims if I let my guard down.

Another of our unwritten traditions is that, until our kids are teen-agers, I will put them to bed every night possible. We talk, read, sing, and pray together. Following a tradition set by my own father, I take that opportunity too to say nice things about their mother. "Don't we have a great Mom? Isn't she good to us? Do you have any idea how much she loves you? Do you know she works at least twice as hard as Daddy? Aren't you proud that she always looks so nice?"

A Rose by Any Other Name

I thought of how important the strength of a marriage is to children when I saw a quote by Pete Rose, Jr., recently. The betting scandal his father was in meant little to Petey. He still dwelt on his parents' years-old divorce. His father was remarried with a new child and another on the way. His mother was tending bar in Cincinnati.

Petey is a better-than-average big league prospect himself, and athletes at that stage in their careers are usually single-minded and driven. Yet Petey said something like this: "I would trade whatever future I have in big league baseball to see my parents get back together."*

It was as if he hadn't read the papers, didn't know the truth about his parents' marriage. Pete, Sr. had such an incredible reputation for chasing women, and such nasty, impossible-to-take-back things had been said by each about the other, that no one would give two cents for the possibility of any civility, let alone a reconciliation. And with Pete, Sr., remarried, there's no chance.

Yet that comment from little Pete, if he were my son, would haunt me to my grave.

Love Me, Love My Mom

The following statement has been attributed to everybody from Howard Hendricks and Josh McDowell to James Dobson. It probably preceded all three, but it remains a truism: The most important thing a father can do for his children is to love their mother. When we know that one

* Mike Bass, *Cincinnati Post* as printed in the *Chicago Tribune*.

of the great fears of childhood is abandonment, we can only imagine the impact of a broken marriage on a child.

May "the Vorce" Not Be With You

Several years ago *Campus Life* magazine ran a story about "The Vorce," which was a child's misunderstanding of the word *divorce.* A child in the story said that sometimes people even talk about "The the vorce," which she couldn't understand at all. All she knew was that anytime anyone ever talked about *the vorce* or *the the vorce*, it was sad and bad news. It had something to do with Mommy and Daddy, and she didn't like the vorce.*

It reminded me of a little girl I knew when I was seven. I thought she was the sweetest, cutest four-year-old I had ever seen. Because of our difference in age I didn't see much of her during the next few years, but by the time she was nine she was a sad little creature with a drawn face and red eyes. The only thing she would tell her Sunday school teacher was that she was afraid of the vorce. Her teacher thought she meant some kind of force, but soon the truth came out.

Her parents were leaders in the church and seemed to have an idyllic family with several children, including a couple of adoptees. More than once, however, the children had been awakened in the night to their parents' arguing, even yelling and screaming. That was when this pretty little girl had first heard about the vorce. Her mother was pleading with her father not to get the vorce. Whatever it was, the little girl knew it was bad.

---

* M. J. Amft, "The Vorce and Other Questions," *Campus Life* (January 1978): 43f.

Divorcees will tell you that children are resilient, that a divorce is better for a child than a bad marriage. But experts in child psychology tell a different story. Some kids who bottle up their emotions and pretend it's all right to be shuttled back and forth between parents and cities, sometimes by air, grow up emotional wrecks. They're unable to trust or fully love anyone. They fear rejection, suffer low self-esteem, careen in and out of doomed marriages, and leave in their wakes children just like themselves.

This is the generation that is growing up now. What will family reunions and family trees look like at the turn of the century? What kinds of adults will be running our corporations, leading our government, pioneering technological progress?

We can grow paranoid, I guess, but with more than half of all new marriages ending in divorce and wreaking havoc on the minds and emotions of that many children, mayhem seems the only prognosis. The only way to ensure a future with stable marriages and home lives is to begin strengthening our families now. Give kids a model of love and caring and interdependence. Show them what it means to make and keep a commitment, to set your course on a lifetime of love with no wavering, no excuses, and no me-first philosophies.

Don't fall prey to the Quality Time trap or to the myth that kids are resilient and will be better off in two halves of a broken home. Most children of divorce are just like Pete Rose, Jr. They'd give up everything else important in their lives if only their parents would get back together. Make a decision. Set a course. Carve out the time it takes to devote to your wife and children, and plant a hedge that will protect you and her and them from the devastation of a broken home.

PART THREE

WHAT HEDGES CAN DO FOR YOUR FAMILY

Verbalizing the hedges in your marriage will give your spouse and your children a deep sense of love and security.

THIRTEEN

EVERYBODY LOVES A LOVE STORY

It's important to share with our spouses and children the memories of our own courtship, marriage, and honeymoon.

It's never too late to try to recall the memories of your early love, but the longer you go without doing it, the easier it is to forget important details. By telling our stories over and over through the years, we solidify in our minds the things that attracted us to our mates in the first place. Just as important, our children learn the history of the relationship. I was always fascinated by the stories my parents told about how they met, fell in love, and stayed true to each other during their engagement, although World War II kept them apart for thirty-four months.

There are various ways of reminding one another and your children of your own love story. Obviously, it's not a good idea to force the story on casual acquaintances or neighbors—unless they ask—but you'd be surprised at how many people are indeed interested: old friends, close relatives, people from church you know well. Trade stories with them. Everybody loves a love story.

I share my own story here only to show you the types of memories you can ferret out to share with your mate. I call it *my* own, rather than *our* own, because every courtship is really two stories, yours and your spouse's. Dianna's story contains parallel elements, of course, but the emphases are her own, and her perspective makes for an account with its own unique interest.

Every time we tell our stories, we remind each other of incidents we hadn't thought of since they occurred in the early 1970s. Every birthday, anniversary, holiday, or no-reason-I-just-felt-like-sending-a-card provides an opportunity for a note or a comment, maybe just a sentence from our wedding vows to share with each other. Repeat a wedding vow in your spouse's ear the next time you kiss hello or good-bye. There's no reason not to celebrate your wedding anniversary every day in some small way. If you have a good marriage, build a hedge around it by celebrating it. Think how unique a gift you have been blessed with in this generation of divorce.

My Story

I had not dated for a year when a friend and his fiancé began telling me of a girl I just had to meet, a classmate of theirs at Fort Wayne (Indiana) Bible College. She was tall and beautiful, they told me. *Oh, sure,* I thought. *That's why she has to resort to blind dates.*

I got a look at her from afar when I visited the campus and saw her in the homecoming court. They were right. She was gorgeous. So much so that I was intimidated. No way I would have dreamed she had a night free, let alone that she would accept a date with me. I figured I'd be wasting my time and pride by asking her out.

"But we've told her about you," my friends said. "She's open to a blind date."

I told them to forget it.

"I've seen her," I said. "She hasn't seen me."

But my interest was piqued. Maybe someday.

Someday came a few months later. They talked me into driving over from Chicago for a double date. Ever the romantic, I started building up the possibilities in my mind. I decided that if anything was to come from this encounter, I would know immediately and would be smitten with her.

The blind date on a Friday night in May 1970 was fine. She was lovely, refined, soft-spoken, smart, likable, and easy to talk to. No whistles, bells, or fireworks. As soon as he got me alone, my friend wanted to know what I thought.

"Fine," I said.

"Just fine?" he asked.

I nodded. "Could you get interested? Try to build something?"

"Nah. I don't know. I don't think so."

"Why not? Something wrong?"

"No. We just didn't click."

"You've had all of one date!"

"Yeah, but I'd know."

"You're crazy."

"Maybe I am."

The next night we doubled again and my reaction was the same. Dianna and I promised to write and I said maybe I would come back again, feeling polite and benevolent. We corresponded occasionally over the next few weeks, and I sensed Dianna was more interested than I was. In fact, if she had not gently pressed the fact that I had said I would come back sometime, I probably wouldn't have.

Dianna told me later that at the wedding of the friends who had introduced us, she sensed my lack of enthusiasm. I was busy in the wedding party and only really spoke to her as she was leaving. For some reason, just before she got into her car, I reached out and touched the tip of her nose. I meant it as a friendly gesture. She took it as the only bit of encouragement she had.

Before I finally drove back to Fort Wayne on July 18, I had the audacity to tell my friend that if everything went the same as before, I was not going to pursue the relationship. "You're crazy," he said again.

This time it would not be a double date. She was going to cook dinner for us at her place and then we would walk around The Landing, an old section of Fort Wayne. I pulled in the driveway and went to the front door. As I rang the bell I could see Dianna through the screen door, heading for the kitchen.

"Come on in," she said. "I have to catch something on the stove."

She flashed a smile as she hurried past, and something happened to me. After two double dates and a brief chat at our friends' wedding, it was love at fourth sight. Dianna says the only difference since I had seen her last was her tan. I don't know what clicked. All I knew was that it was the most dramatic emotion I have ever felt, before or since.

I hardly knew the woman, but I knew beyond a doubt that I would marry her. I don't know how I knew, but I knew it as surely as I knew my own name. I followed her into the kitchen, and I was speechless. I literally couldn't say a word. If she had asked me how the drive was, I would have been able to manage only a nod.

Anyone who knows me knows that being speechless is not one of my common maladies. And Dianna is the opposite. She's most comfortable when someone else is carrying the ball in a conversation. That was one of the things she liked about me—that I enjoyed talking, drawing people out, discussing whatever anyone was interested in.

She acted as if she didn't notice anything unusual, and she uncharacteristically chattered about the chicken, the vegetables, the salad. I watched her slice carrots, thinking, *She is going to do this in our home someday. I'll watch her do this for the rest of my life.* I can't explain it. I just *knew*, and I never wavered.

When I finally spoke, my voice cracked, and I noticed her double-take. I recovered quickly, but what an ordeal that meal was! Dianna grew up on a farm and was a 4-H champion cook, so the food was wonderful. But there I sat trying to make small talk on our third date, all the while hiding my delicious secret: I was going to marry this girl. She had been more interested in me than I in her, and now I had shot past her by light-years.

Dianna and I were impressed by different little things that night. I remember I was impressed that a basically shy girl felt comfortable enough to put her feet up on a chair during the meal. Later, as we strolled The Landing, holding hands for the first time, she was impressed that I wouldn't let her run to the car when it began to rain. She worried about how her hair would look. To me, she would have looked good bald that night.

Later we drove to a park in the center of the city where we walked in the rain. It was one of those nights that nearly every couple has at one time or another in their relationship. We talked of everything, learned of childhood memories, quizzed each other on favorite colors, foods, tastes in clothes, books—anything that came to mind. I was in paradise.

I could hardly contain my secret. I wanted to tell her something, anything, that would alert her that to me this was much, much more than a typical date or even a new relationship. I knew it didn't make any sense, but I also knew to the core of my being that this was it. She would be my wife, and there didn't seem to be anything anyone could do to stop it.

Before I left her for the two-hour drive back to Chicago at midnight, I pretended to be kidding and told her I thought I was falling in love. She thought that was funny, and I was glad I hadn't seriously revealed my heart. By the time I got in the car, sense or not, I was helplessly, haplessly, wholly in love. I thought I had been in love before, but now I knew better.

All the way to Chicago I sang, whistled, talked to myself, and tried to think of someone I could tell. One of my friends worked in an all-night gas station in my home town. I arrived there at two in the morning, grinning from the waist up. I went into the station and sat on a fifty-five-gallon oil drum.

"I want you to be in my wedding," I told him, beginning a three-and-a-half hour rhapsody.

My friend had never seen me like that. He shook his head.

"You've got it bad," he said.

I didn't know how right he was until I climbed down off that oil drum at 5:30 in the morning and realized I'd been sitting in a quarter inch of motor oil the whole time! It had soaked through my seat and down my pant legs, even into my socks, and I hadn't had a clue!

With the morning newspaper between me and my car seat, I arrived home at six o'clock in the morning and peeked into my parents' bedroom. My mother opened one eye.

"You're in love," she said.

She couldn't have paid me a higher compliment. I couldn't get over the fact that it showed, and she hadn't even seen the oil yet.

I didn't sleep for a couple of days, but I did get started on what would become astronomical phone bills over the next several months. I tried as hard as I could not to let my temporary insanity show through, but I was not successful. Dianna didn't know what to make of it, and when she visited Chicago for a weekend, my secret was out. For the next several months, I tried not to make a fool of myself, and she carefully considered this new friend who had started with such ambivalence and was now running ahead of her own feelings.

It was during that period that I discovered the depth of the woman I was already convinced would be my wife. Before long, my infatuation had matured to true love. By September, Dianna shared my feelings and we began to think seriously about the future. In November she suggested a brief moratorium on the relationship. We had known each other such a short time and were talking so seriously of marriage that she wanted to back off for a couple of weeks and sort out her feelings.

I was devastated.

I didn't tell Dianna, but I was convinced she was doing this only because it was the type of thing her friends had done. Worse, I was in dread that she would come to her senses and realize she could do so much better. I believed that if I ever heard from her again it would be in the form of a Dear John letter or a phone call suggesting that we could be just friends.

This was, of course, years before Dr. James Dobson's excellent *Tough Love*, which advises the waiting party in such a relationship to maintain dignity. Part of me wanted to beg and plead and cry and ask how Dianna could do such a thing to a person willing to crawl in front of her for the rest of her life, licking up dirt so she wouldn't have to step in it. Wouldn't that have been a nice example of the kind of man a woman wants as a husband?

I resisted the urge to grovel, but I did do a lot of tearful walking and praying. In retrospect, I see myself as a sniveling weakling who had enough foresight to keep it to myself. But at the time, I was truly in turmoil. I felt that Dianna was meant only for me, that only she could make me happy. I held to the conviction from our fourth meeting that we were meant to be married.

But I had to come to the point with God where I was willing to give her up. I had to get to the place where I conceded that if I truly loved her, then I would want what was best for her. If what was best for Dianna was not me, then that was what I wanted for her. Otherwise, my love was selfish. It was not easy, but after four days in the pits I made that concession in my own mind. I didn't feel much better, and I wouldn't like it if it turned out that way, but I knew I had done the right thing by being willing to accept it.

That night she called.

"Enough of this nonsense," she said. "I miss you. Come when you can."

I was tempted to let her wait a few days, but I drove two hours to see her for half an hour, then drove back home. We married within three months.

I don't begrudge her the four days she needed. I am glad, however, that she didn't need the entire two weeks. I would have been a basket case. Whatever she settled in her mind during those few days has lasted our entire marriage. For whatever grief it caused me then, it has afforded me a wife with no second thoughts.

Peoria?

Clearly, that story is personal and is of real interest only to those involved—a group which includes our children. If we go several months without sharing our story, our sons insist on hearing it. They like to hear of the wedding too, giggling over the account of my father pushing the *play* button rather than the *record* button on his tape recorder at the worst possible moment. While the pastor exhorted us, we were also treated to ten seconds of a business seminar Dad was trying to tape over.

We wrote our own vows, borrowing some ideas from the friends who had introduced us. We promised each other that we would "keep you only unto me," and rather than the morbid, "till death do us part," we used the more upbeat, "for as long as we both shall live, or until Christ, who has saved us by His grace, returns to take us unto Himself forever."

I also vowed to make Dianna laugh, which I have tried to do daily for nearly two decades. (If I've failed by the end of the day, I sometimes resort to swinging from the chandelier.)

We were married in downstate Illinois and left the next day to drive across the country for a job in Washington State, so we spent our first honeymoon night at the Holiday Inn in Peoria. It didn't seem at all funny then, but that gets the biggest smile today when we recount our story.

Tell your story. Tell it to your kids, your friends, your brothers and sisters, but especially to each other. The more your story is implanted in your brain, the more it serves as a hedge against the myriad forces that seek to destroy your marriage. Make your story so familiar that it becomes part of the fabric of your being. It should become a legend that is shared through the generations as you grow a family tree that defies all odds and boasts marriage after marriage of stability, strength, and longevity.

FOURTEEN

WHEN VICTORY COMES

Something wonderful happens in a relationship when hedges begin to grow.

It's crucial to understand that the hedges I've discussed have been my own, tailor-made for an over-sexed, gregarious, fun-loving, busy person who might otherwise follow his lusts, say things he shouldn't, flirt, forget the most important person in his life, and not spend as much time with his family as he should.

Your weaknesses may be different. Some of them would make me laugh or think you're a nut, as some of mine may have done to you. The important thing is to know yourself, understand the dangers in your weak areas, and do something practical and concrete about them.

The case studies that follow are of two couples who have learned the hard way to plant their own hedges.

Their hedges bear little resemblance to mine. That's the point.

Except in the case of the first couple, names and insignificant details have been changed to protect identities.

Pat and Jill Williams

I was privileged to work with Pat and Jill Williams on a book about their marriage. I met Pat in the early 1970s when he was general manager of the Chicago Bulls professional basketball team and I was a young writer interviewing him for a story. I eventually wrote his biography and then a motivational book with him, but the most significant project we ever hooked up on was *Rekindled*, which became a surprise bestseller and still sells in hardback at this writing, more than four years after its release.

The Williamses still receive an average of a letter a day from some distraught spouse, lamenting the state of his or her marriage, informing Pat and Jill how similar their stories are, and pleading for help. Pat sends me a copy of every letter, and I need to tell you, such correspondence provides one depressing look at the state of the Christian marriage in this country.

Pat and Jill and I have often remarked on the sadness and desperation and also on the remarkable similarity among the letters. They have received hundreds and hundreds of letters, and they are nearly all the same. The husband has ignored the wife, busied himself in his career, and become a cold, uncommunicating partner. The wife has tried everything to get his attention until finally she was ripe for the attentions of someone else and is now involved in an affair.

Sometimes these stories happen the other way around, but that is the typical scenario. The letter to Pat and Jill comes either from a frantic husband who has seen the error of his ways and is willing to do anything to win his wife back, or it comes from the wife who says she knows it's wrong to be having an affair and she feels sorry for her pitiful, blubbering husband, but she has lost her love for him.

Pat and Jill's story is similar, but Jill did not resort to finding someone else. There is a depth of spirituality and character in her that precluded her looking for another man and even eliminated from her mind the possibility of divorcing Pat. She admits, however, that she was terribly vulnerable during the crisis and can't say with certainty that she could have fought off the urge to look to someone else if the circumstances had been just so.

At the time of the predicament, Pat was general manager of the Philadelphia 76ers, one of the premier organizations in the National Basketball Association. He was at the top of his profession—admired, sought after, a speaker, a jogger, a Bible memory freak—in short, the envy of many other wives. Only Jill knew the truth. He was invisible at home, wrapped up in his work, speaking engagements, devotions, and his physical fitness. "Jilly" was the little woman who was to handle the home and provide the ideal environment for him so he could remain at the top of his game.

Pat thought he had a good marriage. His wife was beautiful and talented and a good mother. She was a creative decorator, a good cook, a singer, a violinist—in short, everything a man like Pat could want in a wife.

For years Jill had tried to get Pat's attention. Her methods became more and more drastic as his solutions to her tantrums became more and more predictable. If she crabbed about his lack of attention or demanded to know why he ignored her in public, if she complained about his curtness to her or his condescension, or if she wanted to know why he never touched her except in bed or didn't have time to talk to her for even ten minutes a day, he would quickly take the temperature of the situation. If it looked serious he would apologize, make promises, bring her flowers, take her out to dinner, and see how long that kept her happy.

After ten years, she had had it, and he didn't even suspect it. She dropped the bomb on him one Sunday afternoon in December. He had killed her emotionally, she said. She told him she would not divorce him, would not leave him, but that neither could she guarantee any emotional response to him whatsoever. He had killed every last vestige of love she ever felt for him. She was finished, defeated, deflated, and she couldn't even smile.

It was as if someone had kicked him in the stomach. When he started his promise to turn over a new leaf, she simply went upstairs to bed. He knew this was serious and that no bandage was going to make things right again. He wept, sensing, knowing finally that she was right. He begged for forgiveness from God and for a solution.

Pat was an obsessive, compulsive person, driven to succeed at whatever he set his mind to, whether it meant memorizing a verse of Scripture a day, spending an hour in the Bible each day, jogging six miles a day, building a winning basketball team, or speaking three hundred times a year. He could do anything. And now he decided to put his mind to his marriage. He was ready and willing to do whatever it took not just to salvage it, but also to make it the best it could be. He wept and wept as God brought to his mind dozens of things he should have done over the years. He was reminded of every complaint Jill had registered over the decade, and he filled page after page of a yellow legal pad, determined to change his ways on every point.

God also led him to a book, *Love Life for Every Married Couple* by Ed Wheat, and he memorized the principles that urged him to apply the B.E.S.T. acronym. He was to bless, edify, share, and touch his wife constantly, not just to win her back, but also simply because it was the right thing to do. In fact, Dr. Wheat stipulated in his book that all this activity would not guarantee any response from the hurting spouse. He said, in essence, that the wounded partner may never respond after all the damage that had been done, but these principles applied anyway and should be followed.

Pat was desperate to convince Jill that this was no typical restart. He really meant it this time. He had really heard her. He loved her with all his heart and wanted to prove it. He was so committed to his marriage that everything else in his life paled in comparison, and yet she could not bring herself to respond. She couldn't smile or even speak except in cordial, formal, functional conversation. He got no encouragement, and he said, "It was like looking into the eyes of a dead woman, a woman I had killed."

The story ends happily, of course. Eventually Pat proved himself. God forgave him and gave him the strength to maintain his commitment to this day. Jill finally forgave him and saw life and love return to her being. At the time of their marital crisis seven years ago they had three children. They have since had another of their own and adopted eight more!

You wouldn't think a household with a dozen children in it would be a healthy place for a troubled marriage, but it is. A miraculous transformation has taken place there, all because Pat got the message and planted hedges, albeit almost too late.

He talks to his wife a lot every day.

He spends time with her and with the children. He remembers special days.

They date frequently.

He applies a lot of non-sexual touching.

She has become the center of his life.

It hasn't been a quick fix. He knows he can never let his guard down, never slip into the old patterns. Now that he is president and general manager of a new NBA franchise and the family has moved to Orlando, Florida, the risks and temptations are greater than ever. Yet his resolve is all the stronger. Remember, these were not just leaves he turned over. They were hedges he planted deep in thick, rich soil, and they're growing strong.

Ike and Laurie Vanderay

Ike is a successful independent insurance agent in the South. Laurie worked early in their marriage but became pregnant almost immediately, and they now have five children under age eleven. They were a passionate, exciting couple during their long courtship, but financial setbacks, health problems, and two miscarriages made early married life difficult.

Seven pregnancies in a dozen years have not been a problem for Laurie. She loves babies, was heartbroken over the two losses, and is even interested in maybe having one more. Both Vanderays are very active in their local church, serving in Sunday school and in the choir and on various boards and committees. Ike is also very visible in community affairs for the sake of his business.

Ike has found that Saturdays can be big in his line of work. People who can't see him during the work week will often schedule a Saturday appointment. Laurie pleaded with him to take one day other than Sunday off, so when his business became healthy enough, he announced he was taking Mondays off.

To Laurie, this was heaven. She looked forward to their getting a baby sitter and spending the day together, or having Ike watch the kids while she spent the day shopping and running errands. She had felt so isolated and trapped that she couldn't wait to just get away for a few hours.

There was a breakdown in communications the first time Ike took a Monday off. He agreed to watch the kids for awhile, and she assumed he knew she would be gone most of the day. Many of his clients had not gotten the word of his day off, so he was trying to answer calls and do business over the phone while keeping track of the kids. The longer Laurie was gone, the angrier Ike became.

When she got home, she got an earful. Not only was she not going to have a free baby sitter on his next day off, but he was going golfing all day. His day off, in case she didn't know it, was for his sake, not hers, and that was the way it was going to be.

"When do *I* get a day off?" she whined. It was a mistake to ask that just then, though it was a valid question.

"You get a day off all day every day," he said foolishly. He lived to regret that remark.

When tempers cooled, the Vanderays knew they had a problem. Ike got an answering machine that informed everyone that he was unavailable on Mondays. He pledged to baby-sit from breakfast through lunch on Mondays so Laurie could eat out with friends and get her errands and shopping done. She agreed to let him do whatever he wanted in the afternoon, and if she needed a baby sitter so she could go with him or remain out on her own, that was okay. Monday evenings also became their date nights.

"It revolutionized our marriage," Ike says. "I feel like I'm helping her. I get time to get away and have some fun. She's happier because she gets out, sometimes for the whole day and evening. And even though we each are getting some freedom to do what we want to do, we are also seeing more of each other than ever."

Laurie says Ike seems like the same young, energetic, funny, creative guy she married. "He's less uptight, and we have fun like we used to. We talk like never before. Sometimes we go somewhere before or after dinner, but sometimes we don't. Sometimes we close the restaurant, sitting there gabbing and planning and telling each other everything all evening. We've even been known to go and park!"

Other Hedges

Some couples schedule a breakfast out each week. I know a pastor and two business executives who have regular appointments with their wives booked right onto their calendars, and their secretaries know those dates are inviolate. They don't necessarily tell the callers where their boss will be, but they do know to say, "I'm sorry. That slot is filled."

To a busy man, an appointment with his wife on a regular basis is every bit as much of a hedge as mine are. Spend time talking with your wife. Find out what her deepest needs are, what she really wants and requires from you. Then plant a hedge around that, around her, around you, around your marriage. It'll be the best gardening you've ever done.

ABOUT THE AUTHOR

Jerry B. Jenkins, forty, is vice-president and writer-in-residence at the Moody Bible Institute of Chicago. Among his many published works are biographies of Orel Hershiser, Sammy Tippit, Hank Aaron, Dick Motta, Pat Williams, Paul Anderson, Madeline Manning, Walter Payton, B. J. Thomas, Luis Palau, George Sweeting, Meadowlark Lemon, Christine Wyrtzen, and Deanna McClary.

His adult fiction series (the *Margo Mysteries* and the *Jennifer Grey Mysteries*) have won numerous awards. He has also written *The Operative*, an international espionage thriller. His children's fiction includes the *Baker Street Sports Club*, the *Dallas O'Neil Mysteries*, and the *Bradford Family Adventures*.

Mr. Jenkins is a humorist and frequent writer's conference speaker. He has taught several semesters of graduate school journalism and communications courses.

He and his wife Dianna live with their three children, Dallas, Chad, and Michael, at Three-Son Acres, Beach Park, Illinois.

The typeface for the text of this book is *Goudy Old Style*. Its creator, Frederic W. Goudy, was commissioned by American Type Founders Company to design a new Roman type face. Completed in 1915 and named Goudy Old Style, it was an instant bestseller. However, its designer had sold the design outright to the foundry, so when it became evident that additional versions would be needed to complete the family, the work was done by the foundry's own designer, Morris Benton. From the original design came seven additional weights and variants, all of which sold in great quantity. However, Goudy himself received no additional compensation for them. He later recounted a visit to the foundry with a group of printers, during which the guide stopped at one of the busy casting machines and stated, "Here's where Goudy goes down to posterity, while American Type Founders Company goes down to prosperity."

Substantive Editing:
Michael S. Hyatt

Copy Editing:
Margaret G. Moon

Cover Design:
Kent Puckett Associates, Atlanta, Georgia

Page Composition:
Xerox Ventura Publisher
Printware 720 IQ Laser Printer

Printing and Binding:
Maple-Vail Book Manufacturing Group,
York, Pennsylvania

Dust Jacket Printing:
Weber Graphics, Chicago, Illinois